INTENTION

PRAISE FOR INTENTION

Everything starts with intent. However, when we cow down to our inertia and give intent a miss, we miss out on wonderful transformational journeys, that could have been ours. This book is a wonderful guide, that could help each one of us, to consciously define our transformations, prioritize our needs, identify the cues, harness our natural abilities, and then actively evolve towards what we should really be.

– SANGEETH VARGHESE, MBA
FOUNDER, LEADCAP VENTURES

This book offers you a framework, steps to take, points of attention, advice, and many real-life examples to support you in your journey.

– HENNY PORTMAN
COACH, PORTMAN PM[O] CONSULTANCY

Intention is the best kind of book. A book that teaches you, but doesn't make you feel like you're in class.

– LEE MILLER, JD, MBA
EXECUTIVE COACH

This book is about making a transformation within yourself and living your life with intention. I loved its readability, stories from the heart and practical tips it offered. There was not one thing about it that I disliked! I recommend this book to anyone who feels interested in diving deeper into themselves and getting the motivation and courage to make a positive change within their life. I give it five stars!

– JANA BEDARD
EXECUTIVE, NIKE

If you're looking to make some intentional changes in your life, whether big, small or somewhere in between, Dr. Brooks has written a book that will ensure your success! Not only is the book practical with lots of sound strategies, it can guide you step by step and is for anyone who's looking to make lasting, successful change!

– SOHEE JUN, PHD
AUTHOR, LEADERSHIP EXPERT AND COACH

Dr. **IAN D. BROOKS, MS**
HELPING **YOU** MASTER INTENT

INTENTION

BUILDING CAPABILITES TO
TRANSFORM YOUR STORY

Rhodes Smith Press
14005 Palawan Way, #112, Marina Del Rey, CA 90292

Intention
Building Capabilities to Transform Your Story

ISBN: 978-1-7359750-0-9
1. Personal Development. 2. Transformation. 3. Empowerment. 4. Intention

FIRST EDITION

To my parents, Yolanda and Dwight Brooks.

With this work, I "*…left a bit of my life in the inkstand.*"

— Leo Tolstoy

CONTENTS

PREFACE

I'M IN THE *UNCOMFORTABLE* BUSINESS, with a passion for improving people's stories. I ask clients hard questions to strike a balance between creating opportunities of discomfort so they can experience something new while not pushing *so much* that they shut down.

Many of my clients choose to avoid the discomfort, and, by not doing so, they waste time in areas of little concern or take paths that don't provide the gains they want. Thus, I often spend time clarifying their desires to change, getting them to open up about their choices, and being intentional throughout their transformation journeys even before they begin.

After several years of this cycle, I started to document a framework of how people could get around these misses and offer solutions to focus on new experiences. My aim was to write something that was authentic to the entire change cycle, similar to the coaching process I use if I were to meet them one on one.

When I completed the first version of this book, I did not release it. Instead, I took a break and analyzed it with a fresh pair of eyes, similar to the way I analyze my clients in our initial meetings. Reading that first version, I was searching for what was missing in the content and challenging assumptions behind what I wrote.

I found that it wasn't good. It failed to articulate the discomfort in a way that would enable a reader – and even myself – to utilize the book in a way that would be helpful. My writing glossed over the hard questions and didn't touch on my *business*. That self-analysis forced me to open up and become the author this book needed me to be. I had to become uncomfortable in my writing, so you could become uncomfortable in your transformation. It will be uncomfortable, but not unmanageable.

Treat this book as a guide, going at your own pace to transform and absorbing the information you gain over time. I've combined research with fictional and actual events that offer references that you are not alone in your pursuit. Seeing others' experiences through a glass window, as I saw myself as an author to the first version of this book, provides a quiet understanding to help you along your journey.

This book should and will take time. All successful transformations do, when truly addressing the hard questions. That is the intent. It is not designed to be thumbed through, but experienced. When you are ready, I will be with you each step of the way.

Ian D. Brooks PhD, MS

INTENTION

Part I

INTENTION

INTRODUCTION

> *"...it is not the most intellectual of the species that survives; it is not the strongest that survives; but the species that survives is the one that is able best to adapt and adjust to the changing environment in which it finds itself."*
> **—Leon C. Megginson**

OUR GREATEST ABILITY

WHAT IS THE GREATEST ABILITY of humans?

Is it Love? Creativity? Hope? Is it that we sense there is something greater than "ourselves?" What about reproduction or our innate curiosity for all that is possible? Responses vary.

As I reflected on my own answer, it was important to me to consider abilities that were not influenced by the time, place, or circumstances into which we are born – such as the type of family, what century, available technologies, the country in which we live, or even our education.

Equally important, was arriving at an answer that was independent of emotion, personal need, life situation, age, gender, or any influence that could not be transferable to any and every person. This needed to be an attribute that people could control with some thought and planning, but would also happen even subconsciously in allowing for fate and evolution. Similar to death being our inevitable conclusion, what is it that we all inevitably carry with us as an asset in life?

With those considerations in mind, I decided that humanity's greatest advantage may well be *our ability to evolve.*

Humankind went from *Homo Erectus* to Neanderthals to *Homo Sapiens*. We've moved from building fires for cooking food and creating warmth, to electric-powered furnaces. We've gone from rocks and sticks, to hammers, power tools, and even robotics.

Adaptation and survival are the simplest, lowest common denominators of all human action. How do the two relate? Author and management professor Leon C. Megginson noted that, when interpreting Charles Darwin's *On the Origin of Species*, *"the species that survives is the one that's best able to adapt to the changing environment in which it finds itself."* While humanity's behavioral adaptations have occurred gradually over centuries, our personal evolution leaves traces of itself in our history and in the stories we have lived, both of which still influence how we transform today.

Our ability to evolve is an essential part of the human experience. Activating that ability allows you to move forward and progress.

While the *capacity* to evolve is innate, taking intentional steps towards transformation, as opposed to the changes that passively occur in our lives over time, requires different capabilities and a mindset that embraces the idea of seeking more. Building such capabilities – behaviors that we possess or understand but may have no experience implementing – impacts our successes when consciously attempting something new. This book was created with the intention of helping you transform your story.

YOUR INTENTION

While our greatest ability is to evolve, evolution can be passive, woven tightly together with the notion that change will happen *to us* – not *because of us*

– if we are prepared to wait long enough. However, true, lasting, meaningful transformations require *purposeful* action that supersedes the inherent limitations of "waiting."

Let's set the stage by defining *intention*. Intention is a state of mind with which an act is done. It's having the mindset, attention, or personal will to concentrate on something or some end or purpose. Intention provides a priority of wants and needs that offers us direction, but it is flexible enough to meet changes in your environment, circumstances, or life.

The journey of how you interpret the content behind the words will shape your expectations. My goal is that this book will cast a light on what and/or how you can evolve to meet those expectations, as well as what doesn't need evolving. Using the process outlined in this book is an experience that will unfold differently each time you put it into action for future transformations.

An example of a planned evolution is my own. My career intention focused on a two-year plan. That was the time I allotted myself to spend at any job prior to moving to a new one. Before considering any role, I identified what I wanted to learn in that new role as well as what I could contribute. This created a focus for how to spend my time – learning and honing skills necessary for mastery and/or future advancement prior to moving on.

Upon completing one year in the role, I assessed what I learned, what I needed to refine, and what skills to develop further over the next six months. Once hitting the 18-month benchmark, I reflected on what experiences I wanted next and the types of roles that may allow for them.

The two-year plan was not set in stone, but rather offered purposeful direction. Some roles lasted longer than two years, based on whether or not I felt what I needed to learn could be acquired in the existing role or if that learning would be better fulfilled through a new position. While always pursuing the desire to learn more, I allowed for the fact that opportunities rarely present themselves "on schedule." Thus, I could leave before completing a two-year window. My goal was consistent – each experience should build upon my established foundation of knowledge and expertise.

Using this as my guiding principle, my career spanned many organizations, roles, and experiences that I have cherished. While I had clarity of my purpose going in, I also experienced additional learning and unintentional results for which I could not have planned.

Irrespective of what sparked your reason to transform, intention is your management of it's response. The goal here is to set the boundaries around your intention. This process will be strategic, and offer-structure for achieving a goal while allowing for flexibility in discovering the path to get there. Purposeful evolution considers your current abilities, how they may serve your goal, and acknowledges what you also need to develop to meet your targets. The process in this book will act as a foundation to achieve goals not only for today but also those yet to come.

CAPABILITIES

Transformations tap into our greatest ability: to evolve. When operating with intention, however, transformations also require building new *capabilities*. These are sets of skills or behaviors that you have the *potential* to perform, and at certain levels. Capabilities provide the infrastructure to address evolving targets. Because targets frequently change over time, you are continuously refining your capabilities over time. This minimizes the need for having to perform an overhaul in the future.

Originated from the Social Cognitive Theory developed by psychologist Albert Bandura, there are <u>five human capabilities that contribute to development and behavior</u>:

» *Symbolism* – Symbols offer meaning and structure in your life from past experiences.
» *Forethought/Planning* – Giving thought to what you want and then setting a course of action.
» *Vicarious Learning* – Learning from others via observation, discussion, or other means.
» *Personal Regulation* – Having control over your emotions and actions.
» *Reflection* – Analyzing your experiences, then adjusting.

Each of these capabilities are influenced by:
» *Personal Choice* – Realizing you have the freedom to achieve well-being on your own terms.
» *Your Goal* – Pursuing targets based on what you value.
» *Opportunity* – Creating moments to utilize your capabilities to develop and evolve.

To be clear, states of well-being are defined as present assessments of current conditions, such as "I am cold," or, "I am nourished," or "I am educated." Examples of creating opportunities for utilizing your skills may include caring for a dog, going for a run, going to class, or going on a date. Thus, capabilities are functions of knowing what is possible, identifying the steps and knowledge to reach those possibilities, then creating opportunities to realize what you value.

You are already equipped with humanity's two greatest abilities – the ability to adapt and the ability to evolve – and you can activate them by tapping into the power of intention. When executed well, intentional actions during transformation lead you closer to your desired self.

This book is about harnessing natural capabilities.

Transformation of your story focuses on strengthening your capabilities across five areas:

The first capability focuses on *Discovery*. The intention is to expand your awareness beyond the challenges presented, exploring deeper into what you wish to solve. The way in which our needs present themselves often mask underlying issues, which results in wasted time or activities that only address surface concerns. The goal of *Discovery* is to uncover previous decisions and frameworks that will influence how you achieve your change.

The second capability focuses on the *Principle of You*. What we identify as targets of change usually overlooks acknowledgement of who we are inherently and the symbols we associate with our pasts. Acknowledging your uniqueness ahead of your transformation uncovers influences from three areas – notably your *environment, your decisions, and your actions*.

Expanding your awareness and exploring yourself provides the foundation for the third capability – *Direction*. Here, you will intentionally plan a transformation *specific to you* and practice forethought toward developing behaviors and routines that will move you forward.

You will build your plan based on what you want, acknowledging what you're willing and unwilling to do. Then, identifying those behaviors, you will apply your capabilities towards achieving certain goals. In addition, you'll consider the ways current routines and your environment either help or hinder your ability to transform.

The first three capabilities ask that you take a strategic view of who you are, your target(s), and how you plan to evolve with intention. This is where you will provide forethought as a function of specific planning – a step often missed – prior to taking action.

Realizing the steps in transforming your story starts with the fourth capability – *Experience*. This capability is usually where changes first become noticeable. It focuses on acting in the now and regulating emotions that may arise in the moment.

While done to some extent throughout the process, the <u>final capability –
Attunement</u> – allows you to reflect on progress and learn from adjustments
for building consistency in new behaviors.

The combination of each capability brings clarity of path and the motivation
that comes from purposeful action, with the intention to execute whatever "evolution" you hope to achieve. You will also find drawings integrated
throughout the book that give emphasis to points in each section to recall
during your journey.

Although described in a linear fashion, know that transformations are not so
neat and predictable. Your transformation will ebb and flow. Further, transformational success is based on the collection of changes and decisions you
make each moment – hourly, daily, weekly, or monthly – which lead to outcomes and *sustained abilities*. Thus, the actions of eating well, exercising regularly, getting enough sleep, etc. lead to the goal of achieving an optimal weight
and staying there. It becomes a newly adopted lifestyle, a new way of life.

Each of these five capabilities, coupled with your continuous ability to act on
them, will result in a transformed story.

COMPARING CHANGE AND TRANSFORMATION

The words "change" and "transformation" are often used interchangeably.
While there are similarities, there are also important differences between the
two terms. Before comparing the two, it is important to note that there is no
universally agreed-upon version of change and transformation. Some may
say they are going through changes, while others may describe the same experience as going through a transformation. For purposes of shared understanding, I'll distinguish the two as follows:

» Changes are the *individual actions* that lead to bigger behavioral outcomes
   and results. Changes tend to be *event-driven*.
» Transformations are the *collection* of changes that lead to a broader outcome. Thus, the actions become *a newly adopted lifestyle, a new way of life*.

Changes do not inherently mean loss. However, it may feel that way because
our bodies and minds experience discomfort during change as we take steps
forward. The discomfort comes because the actions we are taking are new.

In contrast, transformations are about *shifting*. When shifting, we're moving
from one place to another in small increments that unfold along a new path.
When we shift our mind and our actions, on a consistent basis, this is when

we transform. Further, transformations are a combination of an internal process (emotion) and coming to terms with the details of the new situations that changes bring.

As an example, consider the transformation of a caterpillar into a butterfly. The caterpillar has evolved from something it once was (caterpillar) to something that has a new form, identity, and life (butterfly).

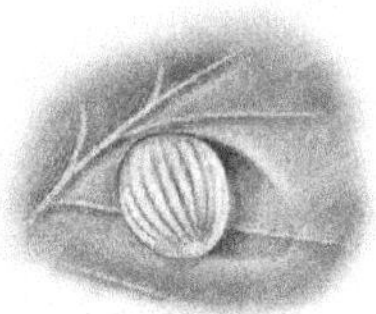

Transformations take time. Step by step, until a new reality is revealed.

Like a caterpillar becoming a butterfly, I'm asking you to *transform*.

KEEP YOUR P.A.C.E.

There is an emotional pull to address your immediate points of interest *now*. It is important to realize, however, that the building and refinement of your capabilities will occur over time, not in a singular moment. To build capabilities over time, transformation requires management of your P.A.C.E.

P.A.C.E. is an acronym in which:

» **P is for <u>Patience</u>** – There are no shortcuts when investing in you. You did not arrive at the desire to transform overnight. So, be patient with yourself. There will be peaks and valleys to manage. Keep being patient.
» **A is for <u>Accountability</u>** – This is your story. While there are those impacted by it or who may influence it, your story is your own. Accountability to take action rests with you, not with anyone else.
» **C is for <u>Commitment</u>** – Give yourself a fighting chance at improving your story. Commitment to change starts strong but tapers off as we get into the action phase or start encountering struggles. Your long-term commitment is important for sustaining your transformation and growth.

and

» **E is for <u>Emotions</u>** – The emotional toll (mental and physical) transformations require is exhausting. There will be moments in which you question your emotional fortitude to continue and it is important to recognize your reactions through this journey so you can handle them in a positive manner.

To intentionally manage your P.A.C.E., there are opportunities throughout the book to *Pause, Process,* and *Reflect.* The intent is to create self-awareness of your thoughts through specific questions related to what you've read and then bring into focus what resonates most for you and your story.

There will be times when the emotion from what you discover is daunting and you will rush to quick conclusions. To address these thoughts and manage your P.A.C.E.:

- » **Pause Your Time.** After reading a section, simply stop.
- » **Process and Hone In.** Allow yourself to be in the moment and think through what stood out or what emotions a particular section sparked. Your answers personalize this content for your story. Allow your thoughts to guide your answers, without judgment.
- » **Reflect for Self-Awareness.** Reflect on your answers and the assumptions behind each. This will uncover details that could help or hinder your path forward. Each answer offers a foundation for building your plan, taking action, and/or reviewing progress.

By pausing, processing, and reflecting, you will bring enlightenment to the information you read or your experiences in the moment. It is a time to become attuned with your thoughts, what you've planned, or what you imagine you want to be. This practice establishes a level of grounding-and consistent reflection throughout your transformation.

Your answers offer a glimpse into your beliefs and fosters openness to solutions that are not available when you're stuck in survival mode and simply reacting. This time is meant for you to plunge into listening to everything that comes to you. Forget pre-conceived notions of quality or judgment over your answers.

The more time used to manage your P.A.C.E., the more likely you will have a strong plan and experience success with integrating desired behaviors for your future.

The aims of this book are simple: To use research, examples, your personal experience, and your inherent ability to evolve to consciously transform your story.

Now, at your own P.A.C.E., continue the process toward transforming your story, with *intention*.

Part II

DISCOVERY

EXPAND YOUR AWARENESS

*"All truths are easy to understand once they are discovered.
The point is to discover them."*

—Galileo

WHAT IS YOUR COMPELLING REASON to transform? Your answer can be lost without knowing the minutiae behind your answer.

It's human nature to focus on a perceived priority without considering the context (or background) surrounding the issue. What is often identified as a "visible" target is the result of a prevailing discomfort and/or feeling. Other times, it's your environment forcing change. In either case, you are venturing into unknown territory. The goal is to expand your awareness, by respecting your compelling reason *in regard to who you are*, and to achieve change by *effectively prioritizing your efforts*.

THE CHALKBOARD

We make between two thousand and ten thousand decisions each day!

Some decisions are conscious, while the majority – an estimated 95% – are subconscious. The subconscious is founded on biases formed from past experiences that may hide deeper meaning and purpose. Unmasking the deeper meaning of our past experiences opens a window to fully discover what we hope to transform.

Roger von Oech created the *Creative Whack Pack* – a deck of 64 cards that provide different strategies to increase creative thinking. On one card, the author describes a situation where a teacher walked into a classroom, randomly draws a white "dot" on a chalkboard and asks unknowing high-school students to describe what they see. The class answered that they only see a dot. The teacher notes that when the same exercise was conducted with kindergarteners, they came up with 50 different responses!!

Is it just a 'dot,' or is it something more?

What the kindergarteners were able to see – that the high-school students could not – were the possibilities. The possibilities of the dot could be anything (e.g. a spaceship, sun, moon, space, pebble in water, etc.) if viewed from different perspectives.

Because of the desire to evolve quickly, there is a tendency to align our perspectives with past experiences and ignore any potential alternatives. One could easily rationalize that children are not jaded enough at younger ages, where their dreams and their realities are one and the same; whereas the realties experienced by older children and adults replace dreams with truth. Alex F. Osborn, in his book *Applied Imagination: Principles and Procedures of Creative Problem-Solving*, adds that someone's level of creativity in solving an issue is more related to their *energy* than a lack or abundance of creative ability.

Transformations require certain energy for finding solutions, for digging deeper regarding your perceived "dot." For you, each dot offers the presenting issue, but the blank areas surrounding it offer the foundation that has more relevance for your focus than the dot itself. Your perception of the "dot" is the result of past experiences, decisions and structures. To discover the truth that created how you see any "dot," it's important to alter how you view the chalkboard around it.

Let's not confuse the activity of creativity with passing judgment. Creativity takes information, analyzes it, compares it, rejects some of the information, and creates an idea. Conversely, judgments result from decisions and conclusions based solely on the facts. Judgments create verdicts.

In your journey of transformation, you may get mired in quick resolutions based on what you already know, rather than treating your transformation experience as new. Viewing your challenge through a creative lens for solutions is important. Judgments on possible effectiveness can pigeonhole decisions into old habits, and need to be holstered. Also, be aware that in opening yourself up to new possibilities, you will not know all of the answers. There will be unknowns to manage.

To operate with intention, acknowledge the "dot," while recognizing that there are other factors (i.e. decisions, your environment, etc.) that have led to the "dot's" creation. Those factors may be more pressing to solve than the result you identify in the "dot" itself. In most cases, the perceived "dot" you see today will change based on the possibilities you recognize tomorrow.

...OR SOMETHING

"So here I am. Seeking some direction, or assistance, or something..."

It was the last sentence in Lisa's email to me regarding her state of being stuck and her inquiry about how I might help her through personal coaching. The preceding five paragraphs outlined her impending retirement from a job she held for 25 years, upcoming birthday plans, the scaling up of an independent counseling practice, and how she was leading the idea development and a team of personnel for a new online business venture.

Lisa was clear on the time commitments for her counseling practice, the partnership with her family in leading the new online venture, writing and editing a weekly newsletter, as well as plans for its expansion.

Her email reflected what she wanted from others, but missing was what she wanted from herself. During our initial meeting, I identified my observation and asked, "What do *you* want?" She acknowledged the high level of effort it would take to learn about the new venture along with running it, and she said it brought her continued "challenge and excitement." She discussed her passion for dreaming up ideas and thinking of ways to make things happen. When we came to delegating to others, this is where her plans were fleshed out for execution.

All fine answers, but none were specific to what *she* wanted. Lisa could not detail what she wanted, other than to acknowledge that she was overwhelmed and wanted to feel retired. She could only feel her "dot."

Having an *emotional* pull to do something different, but not knowing what that difference *is* can be difficult. It's hard to narrow your focus, when it seems everything is coming at you all at once. Lisa's emotional reaction was one of initial excitement and determination to achieve her goals, only to later feel overloaded and a sense of falling behind. Other clients, when considering the requirements to change, become paralyzed and unable to move forward.

"DOTS" SHOWN TO US

It was a brisk morning and to minimize time spent in L.A. traffic, we agreed to meet at a local coffee shop. It was an introduction meeting to get to know each other, confirm expectations, and clarify what he wanted to get out of the coaching experience.

As he approached, Mark was relaxed and met me with a warm smile. We began talking, and it was apparent that he was affable and could carry on a conversation. Mark was the Chief Operations Officer of a mid-size company that was doing extremely well. His role was focused on business development, public relations, and being the CEO's sounding board on decisions. During our conversation, Mark mentioned how he had previously supported the CEO (Janet) while at another company, and that he was asked to join her leadership team at the current firm a few years prior.

We then transitioned the discussion to the purpose of our coaching engagement and how we could best partner. "So, how was I selected for coaching?" Mark asked, readily admitting that he was unclear as to the real reason he was assigned a coach.

To answer, I drew from meetings facilitated by a consultant in which Mark and other executives were discussing the organization's growth. I told him, "As you may recall during a portion of the executive planning sessions, the idea of providing coaching for each leader was discussed with the goal of improving leadership skills and employee engagement."

I continued, "While the plan was agreed upon, Janet only wanted three or four of her executives to get coaches to test the process initially." I then outlined how the coaching engagement was centered on building the broader executive team's leadership skills, and how Mark was chosen by Janet to be one of the first leaders to go through the coaching experience, with specific focus on improving engagement throughout the organization, and specifically his team.

In this instance, Janet created Mark's "dot" based on the direction of the organization and feedback from his team. Mark understood his team's concerns as much as his own, given his own lack of clarity of how his overall success was measured and how he and his department aligned to other business areas. It was apparent that not only were we solving actions for his immediate team, we were also expanding to address his personal concerns not originally identified. This offered the foundation of *Discovery*, which Mark and I could plan around. We scheduled our next conversation, and I knew there was more work to be done to meet everyone's "dot."

Sometimes change originates by circumstance (i.e. a divorce, the sale or restructuring of a business, survey results, etc.), with defined targets and actions to be taken. You are not only dealing with the "dot" someone else creates, like Mark, you're also having to address personal challenges in the moment, and other areas that you haven't previously acknowledged.

The objective here is to realize that irrespective of the starting point, it is paramount to discover the open chalkboard space (i.e. other actions, your environment, etc.) that highlights a "dot's" true cause.

PARTIAL AWARENESS

Ultimately, what you see and feel is your "dot" is your *presenting concern*. Your perception is masked in biases and quick references designed to make it easier, faster, or simpler for you to move forward.

Self-deception hides challenges behind your point. *If I could just make more money, if I stop smoking, or if my kids liked me more – then everything would be perfect.* It's as if that one thing is holding you back and with one solution, everything will be fine.

Your story is not defined by only one decision, one action, or one "dot."

When focused on the "dot," you omit the *Discovery* of the "chalkboard" surrounding it, and may miss information that could inform clear decisions. You can jump to conclusions, disregard your feelings and wants, and act on impulse. This often results in taking more effort in the long run to correct issues or creates outcomes that come back to haunt you.

Transformation doesn't consist of just one thing; nor does it suggest that everything about you needs correction. It does mean that there are parts of your story that are working well and other areas that may prevent you from achieving your desired goal.

Partial awareness is related to the vulnerability associated with changing. It doesn't mean that what you are experiencing isn't true or valid. It does mean there is more. And the more actions that are uncovered, the more each action can feel like a boulder to move, with its own challenges and unique effort to solve.

Let me show you how partial awareness may play out. In a work situation, I asked my team to identify process areas that were slowing their ability to be efficient. I consolidated their individual feedback, and then asked them to rank the top five issues from that list.

When the top five were ranked, I broke the team into groups aligned to those issues and asked each group to develop a plan associated with their respective topic. For context, I provided them with a guide on how to identify and manage their changes and scheduled a check-in two weeks later so they could discuss their progress.

Similar to my clients, the individual teams jumped directly into solving the issue prior to understanding the context of how the issue came to be or how the solutions impacted others.

During the initial check-in with each team, as they proudly announced their solutions, I asked them about their assumptions based on their solutions.

The more questions I asked about the background and assumptions around the issue, the more quickly their solutions became obsolete as they were discovering that other activities were driving the pain points.

In starting their projects without *Discovery*, they arrived at results that delivered minimal impact. Similar to these teams, we see the challenges in our life, and use our biases of what we perceive we need to accomplish in order to complete the exercise of getting things done. But, again, the impact can be minimal, as we are not seeing the wider "chalkboard."

The lesson for my team, as it is for you, is to expand your awareness.

<u>EXPANDING YOUR AWARENESS</u>

Analysis uncovers clues for the real reasons behind your needed changes, and it increases the speed with which you can address the true nature of your transformation. In a work or personal environment, the analysis can come from feedback from others, your emotions, and your environment.

Clues offer insight into what is known, related information, or new facts about our experiences. *Known Facts* are those that are readily available and are directly related to the desired outcome. *Related Facts* can be more helpful than Known Facts, as they are the pieces that will support the foundation of what you are seeking to change. You will receive *New Facts* throughout your transformation and must adjust your facts in the moment based on what you didn't know before.

Expansion of your awareness does not mean diminishment of what you feel or know. It does mean "Yes, and..." Starting with "*yes*" acknowledges what you immediately perceive is true, while also allowing for the possibility that there is – likely – more. It answers "What else is there?"

The goal is to discover answers that offer descriptions (that are informative) NOT justifications (that tend to be emotional reactions). When searching for the causes, there is a sense of asking the question "Why?"

Historically, business organizations have coached employees on *The 5 Whys* methodology. Quickly explained, *The 5 Whys* is a technique to get to the root cause of a problem. It starts with a problem. Then participants ask "Why?" and then note the cause on a diagram. For each cause, "Why" is asked again and noted, linked to the previous answer. Participants continue to ask "Why" until no more answers can be suggested. Once it becomes difficult to respond to "Why" the probable cause may have been identified. This usually occurs within five instances of asking "Why."

This is good in business and process-driven environments, where a team answers *The 5 Whys* from the perspective of customers or end users (which are typically not the ones providing the answers). Asking *why* questions, when there is no emotional ownership of the responses, is easy, and it is best used in a work environment or one in which the questioner sits in a position of authority in the group hierarchy.

This is not the case when transforming your own story. During my clinical psychology program, it was noted that therapists should rarely (if ever – depending on the client) ask the question "Why?" Miller, Wackman, Nunnally, and Miller, in their book *Connecting With Self and Others*, state that the rationale for avoiding "why" questions is that they prompt an *emotional* response counter to the objective of getting to *reasons*.

"Why" questions require people to respond based on personal decisions, emotions, or actions. Thus, responders are placed in the position of defending themselves, rather than a place of being open to a discussion regarding "reasons."

When asking yourself or others about the "why" behind personal decisions, by the time you get to the third "Why" (if not sooner), you will see a change. This will come in the form of the responder's demeanor, in their tone, in their body language, and likely differences in the answers. As an example, think about inquisitive children who ask their parents "Why," and how their parents' body language, tone of voice, and responses start to change...one from a sense of amusement and explanation, to one of "because I said so." At that moment of "saying so,'" the possibilities of a productive conversation have been shut down.

THE TEST

As an exercise, test the following with your significant other, a co-worker, or a friend. Get them into a conversation on a topic that they have a personal stake in, where they made a choice/took some action. Ask them: Why did do you that?" or "Why do you feel that way?" Remember, asking whether or not a process is efficient would not generate the same level of emotional reaction to the question "why," in the same way that a question that asks why they decided to scream at someone during a conversation.

My intention is to challenge the assumptions behind your "dot." Expanding personal awareness requires vulnerability, being able to ask questions without judgment, and being open to the path the answers bring so you are solving the real issues – not resolving for changes.

It starts with acknowledging what you are experiencing – as it is your truth – then expanding your awareness by asking *"Yes, and..."* Consider, in order for a statement to be true, what have you assumed? What descriptions offer facts supporting that assumption? With those facts, what are you assuming about those answers? (You will explore this in specific detail shortly.) You're answering "What do I see/feel?" and "How did I know?" Instead of an exhaustive analysis, identify both the foundational and fundamental facts impacting your story.

Discover the reasons behind the cause and be careful with the use of the question "Why?"

Discovery is designed to help you expand beyond your immediate focal point. Your immediate "dot" is what you feel is your immediate concern. However, like on the chalkboard, your "dot" is nothing more than a reflection of the background around it.

Your intention is to discover deeper truths – "Yes, ands" – that mask your true targets of transformation. Remember, it was ultimately the kindergarteners' ability to see the blank area of the chalkboard – rather than focusing solely on the "dot" as the high schoolers did – that created their many differing mental pictures. You're being asked to pull the issue apart, and get a clearer view of the chalkboard.

The stories of Mark and Lisa are not unique to them. Indeed, they highlight specific challenges you are likely to face when asked to recognize the "dot." In Lisa's case, she inherently knew that something was "off," and could feel it. Her "dot" was not clear and she needed to explore what that meant. Mark had to recognize the mixture of the "dot" formed by Janet, those created by his staff, and – as he tried to see it for himself – his own view of the "chalkboard."

Your motivation should be to expand your awareness beyond what you see, and take steps towards discovering what truly needs solving – in what order and to what end.

To create this level of clarity, ask yourself:

1. What is your perceived need to change or alter your story?
   a.   If you're less clear on what needs to change, what emotions are driving your discomfort?

2. Based on this need or perceptions, what factors – such as how others react, the result you're receiving now or will in the future, or how you feel – support your assumption that you need to change?
   a.   When considering what you want to change about yourself, what are you assuming about you, the situation, or about the impact of others?
   b.   What is your "Yes, and..." to this assumption?
       Once you have your initial answer(s), ask yourself, for those statements to be true, what are you assuming? How do you know these assumptions are true?
       For the next answer(s), ask what you are assuming in order for *those* statements to be true.

3. What behavioral theme or themes come up through your responses that cut across your current situation and others in your life?

If you find yourself asking yourself *Why* questions, try to restate the question to *Who*, *What*, *Where*, *When*, or *How*.

4. As a result of your themes, which of them most resonates with you to start with first?

This is your priority.

You may discover multiple reasons calling for you to transform (some dots created for you, along with others you created yourself). Life offers many priorities, yet the focus of your target involves your individual development.

You cannot effectively hit multiple targets at one time. It actually demonstrates a lack of clarity surrounding what you truly want. So, find a transformative target that resonates the most based on your current need, and make that your priority.

Transformations are fraught with unclear directions and feelings that let us know something is off. Sometimes merely knowing the true issue is the solution and no other actions are needed. Starting your transformation by readdressing your "need for change" from the outset will help you determine where you are and how best to move forward.

Remember: Own your P.A.C.E. with *Intention*.

Part III.

THE PRINCIPLE OF YOU

YOU

"Don't judge the book based on the chapter you walked in on."
— **Anonymous**

YOU HAVE AN INGRAINED WAY of approaching life and habitual actions that you rely upon. The reliance on these actions is heightened during periods of change or unexpected events. You may even find those actions don't work in certain situations, or they only serve to keep you where you are – which can go against the story you're hoping to evolve through in order to transform.

Confronting truths about your story and the effects on your transformation is where most people are not living up to their ability. Instead they're remaining with their defiant selves, sticking to what's comfortable, and failing to see themselves for who they are.

This internal focus on you is one of several layers offering complexity based on some truth, blind spots, and self-deception for survival. Author Abe Arkoff, in his book *The Illuminated Life*, noted that self-deception is useful when it's: (a) temporary, (b) reserved for overwhelming situations, and (c) maximizes our positives and minimizes our negatives. Further, self-deception is either intentional or unintentional.

Intentional deception can result from information you consciously withhold or situations that you purposefully misrepresent. *Unintentional deceptions* involve information you feel is unimportant as part of your story, or may come from your blind spots which haven't been recognized as part of impeding your growth.

Self-deception offers a haven to continue your narrative without fear of showing too much about yourself (decisions or behaviors) you wish to avoid.

This part of the book will help you focus on the *"Principle of You."* It is centered on clarifying the current story that shapes you from the history of you – your characters, environment, and choices – and how this impacts your transformation.

THE PRINCIPLE OF YOU

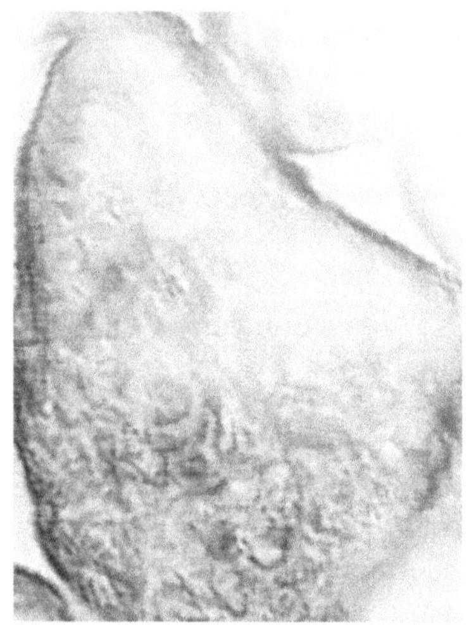

What do you see?

A meteor? A rock? A fossil?

It's a grain of sand.

When viewing one grain of sand with the naked eye, the grain looks very small, even when placed at the tip of a baby's finger. Yet, when that a grain of sand is placed under a microscope, it looks like a boulder.

Still, it's only a grain of sand.

Many grains of sand together create a different picture, like a beach or desert. The picture can be seen as positive – on a beach, in the sun, maybe drinking a cold beverage by the water. The collective image can also be seen as negative – in the middle of nowhere, in the desert with no water, and facing extreme heat.

But you wouldn't know all that without looking at the broader context of that grain of sand. When combined with others, that grain is a part of something. Not to be lost, is that the grain of sand is still a truth unto itself. Unique. Complex. Detailed. Regardless of the surrounding sand. Regardless of its size.

Similar to the grain of sand, your story is more complex than what you want to transform. Your story is built on a foundation of your characters, your environment, and what you are willing to do.

Your actions served a purpose at one time. However, similar to any means of survival, they may have outlived their usefulness and may need to be retired. Further, there may be historical actions, times where you've cut corners simply to reduce discomfort or "get through it," but didn't truly solve the issue.

When uncovering a deeper truth, you are intentionally opening yourself to the vulnerability that comes from recognizing previous decisions, feelings, and actions. This may cause more emotional angst, but it is necessary for your progress.

This is similar to starting the remodeling of a house and finding piping that must be redone according to code. What started as a small project is now one which requires far more effort and stress. This doesn't make us weaker, any more than the deficient piping makes a house less stable. It does mean that there will be more work than initially expected in order to effectively transform.

Similar to grains of sand, your challenge is to explore those themes (or grains) within your story (characters, environment, and choices) that may influence your transformation.

YOUR CHARACTERS

How we respond to each of life's experiences and the instincts we rely upon during stress are central to who each of us are as people. These instincts and approaches combine into "characters," add context and reinforce your story.

Characters are not your life circumstances or roles – such as birth order, status in life, you're a mother, a brother, a CEO, or a doctor. Characters are also not attributes – such as I am charismatic or hardworking. All or some of those attributes may be true and may come out in certain situations, but they are not your characters.

Your characters were developed from life experiences and choices that reinforced certain behaviors for survival. Often characters show up unconsciously and during specific situations in your life.

As an example, one of my characters is "Mr. Degree." At an early age, I set a goal to attain a PhD as a source of validation that I was smart enough.

The assumption behind this goal of obtaining a PhD was that it's the highest academic degree you can receive and, presumably, you have to be smart to get one. While I attained my doctorate, I didn't realize that I created a character that intersected other areas of my life.

In addition to the doctorate, I attained a separate master's degree, a personal training certification, and a bartending certificate. Thus, in various ways I validated my worth with degrees or certifications.

Further, I accompanied my "Mr. Degree" character with other characters. "Lego" has a need for connection. "Martyr" takes on burdens for others.

"Say I Can't" reinforces my need to persevere. Together, all these characters create my story!

It's not that my "Mr. Degree" character is wrong or that I shouldn't have received the degrees or certifications. But, for me to move forward with consulting, writing, and coaching, I first had to acknowledge my various characters and determine which were helping or hindering me in moving forward. Then I took action to manage them appropriately.

In another example, I had a client (Steve) whose character was the "Abominable Snowman," taken from an old Bugs Bunny cartoon. In the cartoon, Bugs Bunny and Daffy Duck are on their way to what they thought was Palm Springs, but misdirection from digging underground led them to the Himalayan Mountains. For context, the Himalayan Mountain range is in Asia, while Palm Springs is in the desert of Southern California.

As Bugs and Daffy arrived in the Himalayan Mountains, awaiting them was the Abominable Snowman. The Snowman gave them both disabling hugs, believing he had found pet rabbits. While well intended, his overpowering hugs and pats took away from any positive feelings experienced by his newfound friends. Thus, the Snowman's new targets for affection – Bugs and Daffy – spent the remainder of the cartoon running from him.

Throughout our sessions, Steve and I discovered that his "Abominable Snowman" character detracted from his work and personal goals. He was suffocating his wife and kids, through constant oversight and hounding them for information. As a result, his family was pulling away from him and not communicating. Of course, that caused him to hold on even tighter. Much like the Abominable Snowman!

At work, he took on more assignments, to please his bosses. This undercut his peers, as he attempted to ensure he was seen more favorably. At the same time, Steve's efforts detracted from his ability to get a promotion because he took on more than he could effectively handle, thus impacting his performance.

After several conversations, I called out his character of the Abominable Snowman. I explained how it was detracting from the trust he was trying to build with his family and how it was working against the effectiveness he wanted to demonstrate at work. The acknowledgement of his character allowed us to discuss his actions openly so he could adjust his character to improve his own results.

Some characters are more memorable and influential in your life than others. Just like with my characters and Steve's Abominable Snowman, your characters influence your story. But it's the collection of your characters' actions taken together that influence your story more than any one character alone – despite how prevalent one character may be in comparison to others.

Not to be lost, there may be instances where you've been miscast as a certain character and assume a role that you don't want for yourself. You're "Mr. Crutch" because you play the role of holding others up or you enable certain behaviors in others. Or you're the "Tasmanian Devil" because others may bring out chaos or provoke negative conduct from you when they're around. You're "Julia Childs", as you've become the de facto chef.

What is true about the characters we are and those we assume because of others is that they answer part of the question of "Who am I?" Your characters are anchors for how you act and react.

Relative to your goals, characters may detract from the ability to improve your story and achieve your desired behavioral changes. Understanding those characters that influence your narrative helps contextualize who you were, are, and what could be different in the future.

Work to acknowledge your characters and recognize how your natural tendencies show up when you're stressed or threatened. You never lose your characters; and in the context of transformation, you may need to live above them.

YOUR ENVIRONMENT

Symbols guide our perceptions and rituals based on experiences and choices. Your environment (i.e. people, places, and things) offers a reflection of symbols that give your story routine and meaning. Whether or not you like dogs, going to the dentist, or what it means to be in an intimate relationship are all examples of your environment acting as symbols.

A goal of overcoming the fear of dogs, going to the dentist more regularly, or finding a healthy relationship that fits your values all tap into historical references of how to act or feel, and these references influence our reactions when in those situations.

Familiarity with our environments can distract us from our overall purpose. By changing what you do and expect, you're also changing how you experience the environment.

For some aspects of our environment, it's easy to change. You may have limited interactions between that aspect and your day-to-day life. Other environmental aspects are harder to change, often because their roles in your life have much larger impacts.

Throughout your history, you and the elements of your environment – people, places, and things – have created certain experiences. Going to a bar, for instance, might equate to always having a drink. Going home to visit your parents could mean playing a role similar to the one that you played while still in high school. Being in a personal relationship may represent situations where you are passive and acquiesce to your partner.

Change is hard on your environment since your evolving story can protect some aspects while it challenges others. As you begin to change, it might seem as though your environment is fighting (consciously or unconsciously) to keep you in the place that's most comfortable. And that place may or may not align with where you want to go.

As an example, I played a game in an improv class based on distraction. In this exercise, three individuals sat next to each other in a row with the person in the middle charged with initiating a conversation with the participant on their left. During this conversation, the individual on the far right was tasked with interrupting the person in the middle by asking them a math question.

The person in the middle had to stop the initial conversation to answer the math question and then continue their conversation with the person on their left. The exercise highlighted the redirection our thoughts take when we're focused in one direction, but must stop to address outside distractions.

Within the framework of your transformation, your environments can distract you from our goals, often without notice or much concern for what you're already attempting to do.

In a more serious example, I was working with Terry for several weeks as she prepared to leave a locked ward in a mental health facility. The ward was locked down, whereby clients and staff couldn't get in or out of the area without a key. If a client did leave the locked area, they were escorted to their destinations.

I bring up the ward setting as it offers context to the Terry's experience. It was a controlled in space and time. This environment offered a specific purpose of daily regiment and oversight. Its purpose was to protect and provide focus for her support.

Each day, Terry and I would meet to discuss her progress and the new routines she needed to sustain once she left the ward. We developed a plan she would use to manage her illness and her environment once she left. Terry made significant progress to the point that she was discharged with the hope of not returning.

Unfortunately, she returned over a month later. Upon her return, Terry and I discussed the challenges of her environment. Being home with her parents, the routines she held previously were hard to change, and an inability to manage them effectively played a role in her return. It was sobering to realize just how strong a pull her environment had on her.

Yet, such stories – while not as drastic in impact – occur every day with transformations.

I've worked with others who hired personal trainers and were committed to exercise during the time they paid. However, once the trainer was removed, the commitment to the healthy lifestyle and working out was removed too. Point being, the intentional management of our environment is critical in the management of our stories.

Specifically, change the relationship with your environments (that is, with people, places, or things) that may keep you where you are. Your goal is to consider how your environment will help or hinder your ability to transform.

CHOICE: WHAT ARE YOU WILLING TO DO?

> *"An artist must be free to choose what he does, certainly,*
> *but he must also never be afraid to do what he might choose."*
> **— Langston Hughes**

Nearly everyone wants the opportunity to make decisions to do something, but far fewer want to own the "consequences" that come along with those decisions. It's admirable to have an opinion. However, when you have to realize that opinion comes with imperatives – because it requires ownership and action – it becomes daunting, and many tend to run away or step back from such situations

The actions you decide to take along your journey of transformation are for your choosing.

Choices serve as anchors for action and must be made in order for you to grow. Aligning your choices with your characters and environment, you can begin to clarify what you "will" and "will not" do to transform.

Will reflects motivation and how likely you'll do, much less sustain, new behaviors over time. Psychologist Fritz Perls noted three factors that influence motivation. The first is the *autonomy* to do something different, or the belief you have a say in the what, how, and when of the choices impacting you. Autonomy has little to do with how the change was initiated (i.e. divorce, getting a new boss, manager hires an executive coach for you, etc.), and instead focuses on the choice of how you respond. Autonomy is a reflection of your perceived ownership in something you do.

The second factor in motivation is having confidence that you're *competent* to accomplish a goal. Believing you have or are developing skills to achieve new behaviors reinforces confidence over time. Perceptions of your abilities can determine your targets and overall effort. Thus, building confidence around your capabilities will influence your motivation to experience your complete transformation.

The final factor is *relatedness* – that while you are transforming, there remains a need to be part of a group. It's part of human nature to want to remain connected with others. Plus, associating with others going through a similar transformation or those who "understand" helps to minimize feelings of isolation.

Each factor represents a portion of motivation that will drive you to do something. To be autonomous is the ownership of the choice, and your actions will allow you to motivate your true self. Knowing you have the skills to accomplish your goal or the right support to move forward offers additional motivation.

When transforming, you must be willing to lose parts of your current infrastructure to move forward. You have to decide if you want to live with things the way they are or improve.

Meanwhile, you may feel you are stuck based on previous decisions. Perhaps the decisions you are making now may challenge previous decisions, creating a sense of being overwhelmed. For instance, a decision to seek a new job may be influenced by a previous decision to have a stay-at-home partner and be the sole source of income. Further, the choices and risks for a married person with children to do something different can be different than for a person who is single, with no children, who wants to achieve the same goal.

Decisions layer upon previous decisions to create a story. As you are making new decisions regarding your narrative, you have to reconcile previous decisions that no longer align with your new direction and require attention. You have to be willing to anchor on your current choices and discover your new path.

Your decisions stack upon each other to build the structure of yourself. They are often more connected than you realize until you begin shifting things. Understand your connectivity.

Recall the story of Lisa who recently retired and was "overwhelmed" with balancing retired life, the new online project, and her therapy business. We discussed ways in which she could manage the emotions and actions associated in minimizing being overwhelmed, while maintaining a perspective of being retired.

With her goal in mind, I asked Lisa, "What are you willing to give up doing?" She responded the way I expected, as someone who did not want to give up control. While earlier she indicated an interest in delegating, her perspective changed when confronted from a different direction.

> *"Well, I don't want to give up my free time. I have to set the strategy for the organization so it can grow. And I have my therapy clients, who I cannot let go and that helps fund the activities necessary to get the business started."*

Lisa was clear on what she didn't want to give up but couldn't articulate what she could. Consequently, it was more difficult for her to transform her feeling of being overwhelmed. Recall from earlier, she stated she was willing to delegate. What she said she was willing to do in a casual conversation was drastically different and became more clearly distinct as we began discussing her *will* and *wants*.

Also of note about Lisa is her backstory. For the past 25 years, she worked in the collegiate school system, developing process strategies and then handing them off to others to implement. Lisa's behavior reflected her character and how in previous choices, she was in control of the direction, while others went and executed. So, Lisa being overwhelmed was as much about her balance of work as it was about relinquishing some of the very skills that made her successful.

Based on her willingness to still do everything she planned, we charted a course to manage her time more effectively and to better delegate to others. Ultimately Lisa's "will" to change her feeling of being overwhelmed through delegation, had to factor in what actions she "would not" give up.

Also, for every decision made, there are corresponding decisions and impacts for consideration. A decision to delegate must be met with confidence in others who will accept responsibility for subsequent steps or tasks. Are they (the delegates) prepared to handle the work? How clear am I in my messaging, direction, and expectations?

Conversely, there are decisions each of us make individually that derail our goals. I was speaking to a colleague (Tanya) about her weight-loss goals and the conversation turned to her eating habits. She noted that she bought two gallons of milk each week and had a routine of drinking several glasses in the middle of the night. Factoring in milk's high sugar content, drinking a glass in the middle of the night, then going back to sleep meant this was one way she was derailed her weight-loss goals. When pressed to alter this behavior, Tanya noted that she couldn't do it.

Choices are not always autonomous. There may be influences that govern what you decide to do. There can be people, places, and things in your life that should be altered or experienced differently, but you may consciously choose not to change them.

Also, transformations do not occur in a vacuum and there will be times when your decisions are influenced by personal needs and those who are dependent on you. Further, not all decisions are equal, as some carry more weight than others based on their consequences. Because of these consequences, there may be a negative impact on others or that you cannot undo. This influences your choices and willingness.

That is perfectly ok.

Whatever you decide, know that just as you can own a decision to do something today, you can also own the decision to do something different tomorrow.

Own the choice with the best information you have, plan around it, and move forward.

A CONFORMIST VIEW OF CHANGE: MIRRORING OTHERS

Commonality in knowing *is not* commonality of the impact of experience.

"I want to look like that."

The words shot through my ears as I turned to see a woman talking to a personal trainer and pointing to another gym member walking by.

Our lives are pressured to change, but we conform to what others have done because of our desire to be like them. It's a unique conundrum where our individuality is lauded – only to the extent that you get "likes." This fosters a cycle of similarity. During transformations, such cycles are problematic unless they are effectively managed.

Our observational learning started as children, where paying attention to others reinforced what was right and wrong in our worlds and made it easier to adapt and develop. As adults, this approach reduces trial and error, or helps when our time and energy is limited. Thus, we view others as guides for what's possible and as sources of increased learning.

"Mirroring" can be appropriate, but personal transformations need more consideration of your own story. Without the context of characters or history (which you just explored), comparisons mask how someone achieved a result and the series of choices they have made to arrive at that outcome. Transformations are rarely experienced as "paint by numbers," where following instructions of how others executed a goal will provide you that exact result.

You may *cognitively* understand what someone achieved, but knowing only offers a pane of glass through which to see. What's hard to articulate is the emotional impact which varies from person to person, even with similar experiences. This emotional awareness creates your compelling reason to transform.

This dynamic is the reason protests of lower classes of society, while supported by those from higher classes, are cyclical. Higher classes cognitively know what is morally right, but insight is usually surrounded by an event. Whereas, lower classes fight the morality fight every day – through experience. That doesn't mean the fight shouldn't continue… It does mean cognitively knowing something is different than actually living it.

At an individual level, modeling others assumes similar histories, environments, and considerations when attempting change, as well as assuming similar starting places and *wills* to transform. Yet, the steps and moment-to-moment choices for two individuals who have similar goals are often quite different.

As E.E. Cummings wrote:

> *"To be nobody but yourself in a world which is doing its best, night and day,*
> *to make you everybody else, means to fight the hardest battle which*
> *any human being can fight and never stop fighting…"*

To be clear, "mirroring" inspires action, yet there is so much hidden through your compelling personal experience that cannot be captured through the reflection of another person's mirror. The intention is not for you to ignore others' actions; rather, it is to understand how others achieved a goal and integrate actions that fit you.

This is your time to master your personal design studio and reinvent your story.

PART III SUMMARY – THE PRINCIPLE OF YOU
OPERATE WITH INTENTION: PAUSE. PROCESS. REFLECT.

"When you know who you are and what kind of person you want to be, you'll know what to do."

— Unknown

The *Principle of You* explores how components of your life (grains of sand), characters, and choices influence your transformation. It expands your sense of identity beyond your history and environment in a way that creates clarity on how to move forward. You're building your capability to assess the impact of symbols in your life (conscious – what you're willing to do, and unconscious – your characters) which may require reconciliation or simply acceptance for you to move forward. Remember, you cannot judge your starting place of transformation *based on the chapter in which you walked in.*

In digging deeper, you may be feeling uneasy and want to start the change immediately. Know that this exploration is starting your transformation process.

The core of who you are will likely not change, but offer a reference to manage as you progress through your transformation. As you become clearer on the principles that influence you and your transformation, consider:

YOUR CHARACTERS

1. Who are the characters that influence your story?
   a. Remember, your characters are not a prescribed category – such as race, gender, job title, brother, etc. – but the person you exhibit – such as Abominable Snowman, Mr. Degree, Mr. Rogers (because you want to be liked), Julia Childs, etc.

2. In what situations – such as how you react in relationships, when you are asked to follow, in new situations or when you are challenged – do your characters typically present themselves?

3. Relative to your transformation, which of your characters will help/hinder you in achieving your transformation?
   a. What situations will you need to be mindful of where these characters may present themselves?

Use a few sentences to describe how each of your characters moves, speaks, or responds in specific situations aligned to the story you are transforming.

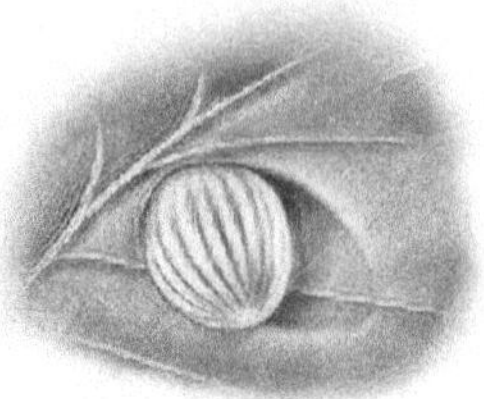

Transformations are not solely about the changes you choose to make. They also involve surroundings and circumstances beyond your own design. Explore and own your past.

YOUR ENVIRONMENT

Reflecting on your priority for transformation, what factors in your environment have an impact on your ability to improve your story? Consider the following:

1. What in your environment (i.e. people, places, things, etc.) may impact your goal to change?

2. What aspects of your environment bring out specific characters you referenced previously?

3. From these, what challenges will your environment have on your ability to improve your story?

4. For those factors that may inhibit your ability to change, how can you alter your interaction with the environment and the reaction it motivates in you?

Acknowledgement of your history, environment, and choices are not once-and-for-all end points. They are conduits, offering you clues as to progress, regression, stalling, and the like. You will need to pay attention to these clues as you move to transform your capabilities.

And finally...

WHAT ARE YOU WILLING TO DO?

With increased clarity of you, leverage your autonomy to do choose to do something different. Ownership of your choices and your actions drives accountability. Your transformation will reflect the boundaries you self-create that either help or hinder your ability to achieve your goals. So:

1. What are you willing to do?

2. What is non-negotiable? (i.e. kids, work, family, etc.)

3. What are you *not* willing to do?

4. Based on what you are willing and not willing to do:
   a.   How might your answers influence your ability to achieve your goal?
   b.   Have you restricted yourself and made it harder for you to achieve your goal based on this/these decisions? (i.e. similar to Lisa)

5. What are some of the unintentional consequences that may result from what you are not willing to do to impact your story?

This transformation story is yours, and not the story of anyone else. Continue to be your author and actor. You will continue to learn about yourself through this journey. Move at your own P.A.C.E. and continue to live your life as though you know yourself.

With *Intention*.

Part IV

DIRECTION

PLANNING YOUR INTENTION

"If passion drives you, let reason hold the reins."
— Benjamin Franklin

33%

THAT IS THE INCREASE IN success rate between those who wrote down their goals versus those who ONLY formulated their outcomes in their head, according to a 2015 study by Gail Matthews.

The results from this study are not much of a shock, as these results are consistent across many studies and experiences. What *is* shocking is the fact that most people *still* do not write down goals or how they plan to achieve them. You're now being asked to marry what you want to achieve with forethought and steps to get there.

I have used this process with previous clients. While it is not always easy, these steps offer clarity of direction and help shape how your transformation will take place.

Planning your intention encompasses six steps in building your foundation for the next month. Initially, it starts with the reintroduction of your priority from *Discovery*. While captured previously, further insight may have altered your perspective of the behaviors you want to address.

The second step, derived from the *Principle of You*, re-clarifies what you are willing to do. Life isn't lived in a box and there will be tradeoffs – in action and energy – throughout your process. Note that what you are willing to do will continuously evolve.

Similar to the previous grains of sand analogy, individual grains – in this case aspects of who you are – appear as boulders on a beach. Each represents an object to move. To manage the experience, the third step is to identify behaviors that have the most benefit toward improving your story. By operating with intent, you will know what to expect and that for which you need to plan. The fourth step frames how you'll measure success to illustrate progress and manage your expectations.

To meet your intent, step five focuses on what level of support you need that can help you achieve consistency or reinforce your new actions. The final step focuses on your return on enjoyment. Because transformations are exhausting, here the purpose is to build in down time where *you're not* thinking or taking steps to transform.

These six steps are designed to synthesize all of the information you've gained to this point and prioritize what's important moving forward.

PLAN AHEAD

Most development plans ask that you choose an appropriate goal and clarify your objective. Yet, what is often missed when creating your plans are the considerations of what the future will be and how to prepare for discomfort when you are experiencing your transformation.

Consider the Future

When building your plan, consider what you need from your future environment and how you must act within it to get the results you want. The future is the world you will be living in, and it forces you to consider how your behaviors will meet or extend past a future point in time.

For instance, planning to develop skills for a job that will not be there in two months or not factoring in getting married in six months when looking at financial goals is not the most productive use of your time.

Focus now on those behaviors that will meet the changing world you're creating or the world that may change around you. This unknown future should not be a threat to you moving forward.

Prepare for Discomfort

"*Listen to what you know instead of what you fear.*"
— Richard Bach

New beginnings expose vulnerability and stir unease. Self-doubt creeps in when dealing with the unknown. Thus, anticipating discomfort assists you when you're planning for new behaviors and environments. In this way, you're prepared to respond to what's new versus reacting to it.

Consider teaching a child how to ride a bike but without training wheels. The joy of riding the bike can be outdone by the child's fears of imbalance when riding with no support, coupled with the result of falling down and getting hurt. The child's discomfort is expressed in panic, crying, or another emotional display. The resulting emotional toll can become negative to the point where they are paralyzed and don't want to ride their bike anymore.

An initial step in riding would be instruction in how they can protect themselves when they feel they are going to fall. Aside from a helmet and kneepads for protection, you could have them practice falling in a soft area where you can teach them to put their feet down or roll. You are coaching them around their fear and not around the act of falling. This approach builds their confidence so that if they do fall, they can more readily get back up and try again to learn a new skill versus focusing on negative consequences.

Does this mean they will not be scared to fall? No, because falling on a soft area is different than falling on a hard one. The physical and emotional pain that comes with scraped knees will need to be managed. But, in this instance, the child is building a capability to manage the fear, while starting to build their capability to bike.

Falls *will* happen. Just as Tour de France cyclists wipe out if they're having difficulty managing their "environments" – or a "character" like "Speed Demon" who moves too fast without acknowledging their surroundings – you too, will fall. It doesn't mean you're inept and incapable of transformation. Rather, this may require some re-examining of the ebb and flows of your "wants" and "wills" experienced through positive and negative experiences.

Similar to physical discomfort, emotional discomfort is just as powerful during transformations. You cannot necessarily plan ahead for emotional reactions, but being self-aware of emotional triggers and reactions is important. The emotion may represent as excitement, anxiety, fear, or some other sign that will provide you information.

In the moment, acknowledgement of your emotion and how it is experienced is not bad. In fact, your ownership allows you to do something with those feelings in a positive way that will allow you to adjust and move forward. In practice, this can be awfully hard sometimes, even when you plan ahead.

Plans can succeed, but not accounting for hiccups along the way causes unnecessary frustration. Anticipating discomfort and building in contingencies for setbacks is as critical as building your original plan.

The intent of anticipating discomfort is to understand how you will own your emotions during situations when you feel out of control while still moving forward.

PLANNING: 6 STEPS TO ORGANIZE YOUR THOUGHTS

Now that you've considered the future and what discomforts you may need to plan around, it's time now to consolidate your actions into six habit-forming steps that will form your plan for the next thirty days.

Step 1: Your Priority

As noted earlier, Alex Osborn, in his book *Applied Imagination*, noted that creative minds take information, analyze it, reject some, and use others as background to create an idea. At this point, you've thought through and captured a lot of information about your narrative.

From this information, the goal now is to create a focus on your target – the most important thing that may be causing your drive to achieve a new goal or address a pain point.

Action:
» From your *Discovery*, write down and reconfirm your priority.

Identifying your most important theme crystallizes where you will place time and energy to build your capabilities.

To make this more explicit, we'll use the following real client examples of their transformations:

Example 1 – Dan: To learn more about myself and become more confident in my gifts, talents, and abilities

Example 2 – Lisa: Reduce the Feeling of Being Overwhelmed

Step 2: What Are You Willing to Do?

Recall from Part III, which asked you to explore the *Principle of You*. You answered, "What are you willing to do?" as an internal discovery of yourself.

It was an exercise in acknowledging your history, characters, and choices. I'm asking you now to pull that information forward to your plan, in acknowledgment of what you will do.

Action:
» From your *Principle of You*, write down and reconfirm what you are willing to do?

(***Note:*** *Bolded content reflects the points discussed in each example.*)

Example 1– Dan: To learn more about myself and become more confident in my gifts, talents, and abilities:

What am I willing to do?
» **Commit to Myself**
» **Give Up Negative Feelings**
» **Work Harder for My Family**

Example 2– Lisa: Reduce the Feeling of Being Overwhelmed:

What am I willing to do?
» **I Want Continued Visibility of the Business**
» **Delegate More Work**
» **Only Work During Specific Hours to Have Balance**

Know, that what you say you are willing to do now in a calm state may be different than when you are in the middle of something uncomfortable. Considering your will now offers an anchor which you can use in your moments of action and when you start measuring progress – which will be discussed later.

Step 3: Operate with Intent

Based on your priority and what you are willing to do, it's now important to identify actions within the next month that will offer the foundation for your transformation.

This part of your journey is where you start aligning your planned actions with intent. This is initially started by reviewing your priority and asking, "In order to achieve it, what am I assuming that I am doing?" This question gets you to consider your transformation from a place of future action and challenge assumptions. You can identify many, but select only two or three.

Following those answers, identify behaviors to take that will allow you to achieve that priority. When identifying your behaviors, target specific actions that will lead to your priority. Here, you want to identify those one or two specific behaviors that you can take.

The intent here when identifying actions is to reduce the amount of decisions you need to make in the moment. Too many actions create feelings of being overwhelmed and shows a lack of clarity.

Action:
» From each of priority, identify those behaviors you want to focus for your transformation over the next month.

From the previous examples, the plans could resemble:

Example 1 – Dan: To learn more about myself and become more confident in my gifts, talents, and abilities

» **Live a Healthier Lifestyle**
» **Workout Regularly**
» **Sign-up for Cooking Class**

» **Foster Productive Work Relationships**
  — Meet with Key Stakeholders

Example 2 – Lisa: Reduce the Feeling of Being Overwhelmed

» **Prioritization of Work**
  — Staff to Correct Levels
  — Refocus of Priorities

» **Engagement of Team**
  — Build Trust in Team

» **Time Management**
  — Set Aside Dedicated Personal Time

Step 4: Reframing Success

> *"Once you hear the details of victory, it is hard to distinguish it from defeat."*
> **—Jean Sartre**

Once you've decided how you will operate with intent, determining your measure of success will provide details of winning and perceived loss.

It's important to frame success in a way that reinforces achievement, while not diminishing your confidence if you fall short.

For each action under operating with intent, moments offer chances to build *consistency* in your behavior. Reframing success on behaviors offers a gray area where you find comfort in your actions and acknowledge the value of the course you're on, even when the end-results haven't actively been experienced yet. Thus, success is the combination of desired actions over time.

Also impacting your success is your confidence about achieving your goal. There is research that supports the notion that believing in your capabilities influences how you decide to use energy toward your behaviors. Positive beliefs reinforce interaction with your environment and your efforts. Conversely, the less confident you are, the less likely you will achieve consistency of your behaviors.

A core component of reframing your success is the focus on your behaviors, not the outcomes it may have on others. For example, someone asked me for advice on how to create a "win/win" scenario with his ex-wife in which she would respect his decisions in how he was co-parenting their daughter.

I suggested he change his conversation to one based on a result not rooted in winning or losing. Results based on either/or scenarios, in which the positive is a win and anything less is a loss, establishes a framework for disappointment. It would be difficult for him to get validation of his parenting decisions from his ex-wife in that kind of situation.

At least he was trying for a win/win. Sometimes people try to resolve conflicts by creating losers. That means that not only must someone be defeated, but the nature of the defeat may force the loser to act in ways that undercut any perceived victory or resolution.

In this case a better approach was to reframe the conversation to focus on benefits to his daughter rather than the emotions of his ex-wife. This removed the emotion and entanglements associated with winning or losing.

Finally, do not lose sight of the idea that reframing success also requires *reestablishing limits*. Establishing limits that reflect what you decided you would do increases the likelihood of finding fulfillment in what you are doing. A lack of limits may indicate not having clear expectations on what you want to achieve, which can result in being overly critical of yourself when goals are not met. The types of boundaries you set depends on your goal and your will. For someone who desire a healthier eating lifestyle, a limit may be to only have one cheat day a week. Another person may have a limit where their goal is losing three pounds in a week, rather than the full twenty pounds someone may want.

When discussing success, you can go overboard in criticism if you haven't set limits or identified consequences that are expected with the choices made. Such an approach causes internal conflict through frustration or anger which derails your motivation to continue.

The intention here is to redefine success so it focuses on your *behaviors* – not specific outcomes – and building of confidence over time. It also ensures you set realistic limits to measure yourself based on what you are committed to doing.

With this mindset, successes will be based on those behaviors that will lead towards achieving what you have set as your priority.

Action:
» Reframe success of your operations of intent to focus on your behaviors rather than their outcomes. List the behaviors you will achieve to get those actions.

Continuing with the behaviors listed previously for the ongoing examples:

Example 1 – Dan: To learn more about myself and become more confident in my gifts, talents, and abilities

» Workout Regularly
— **Walk for 30min a day for 2 weeks, then increase to 45min for the final 2 weeks of the month**

» Sign Up for Cooking Class
— **Sign up for an on-line cooking class to that caters to healthy eating dishes and habits**

» Meet with key Stakeholders
— **Schedule 1:1 time quarterly with key leaders to build better engagement, starting with understanding their needs; First Meetings will be with Legal and Audit Leads**

Example 2 – Lisa: Reduce the Feeling of Being Overwhelmed

» Staff to Correct Levels
— **Work with HR to fill open roles, starting with a chief of staff**

» Refocus of Priorities
— **Review strategic priorities with the executive team for the next year, table those that are not strategic, or fi-**

nance driven; schedule meeting to take place in the next 2 weeks

» Build Trust in My Team
— Meet with the Marketing Lead to take over event attendance and coordination for all in planned events for the remainder of the year

» Set Aside Dedicated Personal Time
— Dedicate every Friday where no meetings occur and address open items
— Block 30 min each morning to review emails and complete charts

These behaviors are what you will use to measure yourself against at the end of the month. Remember, the intention is for you to build consistently and you may need help along the way.

Step 5: Support

Transforming is not solely addressing "How am I doing?" then solving it yourself. You may confuse your commitment with competence and need support through someone teaching you or holding you accountable to move forward. Sometimes, it's addressing "Who do I trust enough to say, 'I need help'?"

When I initially started my business, I joined an accountability group. This set of five uniquely different entrepreneurs met once a month to discuss our individual business plans, goals outside of work specific to family and health, and how each came together for balance and progress. The discussion focused on reaffirming our goals, progress-to-date, the areas in which we were successful, the areas in which we failed, and getting feedback from others in the group in a safe environment. The meetings offered accountability to ensure progress, as well as offer support in a non-judgmental way.

My accountability group focused on my individual actions, but sometimes you need to give support to others to fully appreciate how well you are executing certain behaviors or managing specific changes. When I work with executives, I'm coaching them on how to lead and engage their teams more effectively, and how to improve their effectiveness. This, in turn, often highlights whether or not I am currently succeeding in engaging my own teams or colleagues in an effective manner.

While you are getting support from others, new behaviors only stick when you begin taking your learnings and integrating them into your life. Your support is intended to help you move forward, not act as a crutch where you become dependent on it forever. So, the question becomes:

Action:

» Where might you need support to help advance your journey?

Example 1 – Dan: To learn more about myself and become more confident in my gifts, talents, and abilities

  » **Support**
    — **Find a walking club to join or find neighbors whom I can walk with regularly**
    — **Find a mentor for talent development, either inside of my current organization or with my previous leader**

Example 2 – Lisa: Reduce the Feeling of Being Overwhelmed

  » **Support**
    — **Trust in team to complete work**
    — **Ask husband to remind me when I am working outside of my allotted schedule and keep my time balanced**

Step 6: Return on Enjoyment

We all want happiness. If you ask someone about the reasons they do what they do, the answers will invariably come back to some level of enjoyment.

The final piece of your plan is to consider your *Return on Enjoyment*. The term "Return on Enjoyment" is taken from a group in which I participated regarding business accountability for entrepreneurs. Building in your Return on Enjoyment balances excitement against the unknown.

Return on Enjoyment is the intentional focus on your self-care through this process, aside from any changes you're making. Let's say you're not happy going through the transformation process or the plan doesn't feel like it will help you achieve your goal. In either case, the likelihood of removing your pain points or achieving your goal is reduced, and your new behaviors will be even less likely to be sustained.

Transformation in and of itself is exciting. However, excitement can be replaced with dread, exhaustion, and distrust when you're constantly thinking about your effort to transform. You may begin to loathe the very actions that created the excitement initially. Or you might begin to falter in other areas of your life that require decision-making and a focus that you no longer have available.

This is similar to the '80s toy, Penny Racers. They were toy cars, where a penny was placed in the back of the car to add weight. With your hand, you would pull the car backwards, causing coils in the back tires to "wind up" and create tension. Once you heard the magical "click" sound, indicating the car was at the right tension, you would let the car go to race speedily across the floor. Distance and direction unknown!

For every action, there is an equal and opposite reaction. How have you set aside opportunities to "unwind" from your efforts?

It was a fun toy to play with growing up. Ironically, this "springing into action" behavior is played out through all of human development. Consider grade school children, who are asked to sit still for six to seven hours, to be calm, and "be good students." When the bell chimes to mark the end of the school day, children can be wound up like Penny Racers! They just want to be "set free." Instead? They go home to parents who have been working all day, in their own controlled environments. Who themselves have been asked to "be calm," and now they want their own time to reflect and let loose without having to control someone else. So, what happens? Once the children return home, they let loose by "bouncing off the walls." The children's chaotic activity can test their parents' patience.

The takeaway is that adults, similar to children and Penny Racers, require time to unwind from the mental toll of the restraint required during change.

For the client in example one, the capability she targeted was to foster productive and supportive work relationships. Her "Return on Enjoyment" was planning one activity each week with her children. In the second client example, whose goal was to stop feeling overwhelmed, her *Return on Enjoyment* was daily exercise and setting aside one day to herself.

Building in your *Return on Enjoyment* balances excitement against mental and physical exhaustion so you can become rejuvenated in an intentional manner. Having this time impacts your overall motivation to sustain new actions.

It is not uncommon for those who are going through changes to control those items directly in their focus, but to be less careful about day-to-day decisions. As a result, we can inadvertently rush through decisions or fail to consider them as fully as needed. The goal is to avoid acquiescing to bad decisions in one area based on controlling another.

Some tension is healthy and sometimes necessary throughout transitions. Return on Enjoyment acknowledges that too much tension can be derailing. The intention of Return on Enjoyment is to build in time to let go of your tension by identifying activities that will allow you to unwind, take you away from "overthinking," but not derail your overall path. If such an area exists in your own life, acknowledge it and build such support into your plan.

Action:
» How are you going to give yourself a break to let go?

Incorporating support along with Return on Enjoyment in your plan, may resemble:

Example 1 – Dan: To learn more about myself and become more confident in my gifts, talents, and abilities

» **Return on Enjoyment**
— **Plan 1 activity each week with my two children to build a stronger relationship (together or separately)**

Example 2 – Lisa: Reduce the Feeling of Being Overwhelmed

» **Return on Enjoyment**
— **Go to yoga one time each week.**
— **Act Retired! Schedule Time with Family and Friends**

<u>DAN — MY INTENTION</u>

» **My priority:** To learn more about myself and become more confident in my gifts, talents, and abilities.

WHAT AM I WILLING TO DO?

— Commit to Myself

— Give Up Negative Feelings

— Work Harder for my Family

OPERATING WITH INTENT

— Live a healthier lifestyle

— Workout regularly

— Sign Up for cooking class

— Foster productive work relationships

— Meet with key stakeholders

SUPPORT

— Find a walking club to join or ask my neighbors!
— Find a mentor for talent development either inside my current organization or with my previous leader

REFRAMING SUCCESS

— Workout regularly:
  — Walk for 30 min a day for 2 weeks, then increase to 45 min for the final 2 weeks of the month

— Sign Up for cooking class:
  — Sign up for an online cooking class that caters to healthy eating dishes and habits

— Mett with key skatehodlers:
  — Schedule 1:1 time quarterly with key leaders to build a better engagement, starting with understanding their needs

RETURN ON ENJOYMENT!

— Plan 1 activity with my children to build a stronger relations.

<u>LISA — MY INTENTION</u>

» **My priority:** Reduce my feeling of being overwhelmed.

OPERATE WITH INTENT

— Prioritization of Work:
   — Staff to correct levels
   — Refocus Priorities

ENGAGEMENT OF TEAM

— Build Trust in Team

SUPPORT

— Real-time support - Trust team to do the work!
— Ask husband to remind me when I am working outside
   of my determined schedule

ROE

— Go to yoga 1x a week
— Act retired! Schedule time with family and friends!

<u>LISA — MY INTENTION</u>

» **My priority:** Reduce my feeling of being overwhelmed.

WAIWTD

— I want continued visibility of the business
— Delegate more work?
— Only work during specific hour to have balance

REFRAME SUCCESS

— Staff to Correct Levels
   — Work with HR to fill open positions, starting with the chief of staff

— Refocus Priorities
   — Review priorities for next year with the executive team, schedule meeting to be in within the next 2 weeks

— Build trust in team
   — Meet with Marketing Lead to take over event attendance and coordination of planned events

— Set Aside Personal Time
   — Dedicate Friday morning for no meetings and to address open items
   — Set aside 30 min each morning to review emails and complete charts

POTENTIAL AREAS TO AVOID

Look, plans are great. But one size does not fit all *and* there are tasks or circumstances that we don't initially plan for that may derail progress. Even with sound planning, avoiding tasks that may be futile and planning around noise in your environment can help minimize how much you are derailed in the future.

Tasks of Futility

Survival and transformations are built on the intentional focus of action and the conscious management of activities. What flies in the face of your most important thing are "Tasks of Futility."

These tasks occur when we don't properly align our behaviors with our intended outcomes. Tasks of Futility are different than procrastination.

Procrastination, as defined by Webster, is "the action of delaying or postponing something." With procrastination, you may know you need to be doing something, however you haven't yet started doing it.

Tasks of Futility, on the other hand, are activities you already planned or started, believing they would lead you closer to your intended goal. While well intended, these activities offer no measurable advantage for doing them.

Typically, tasks of futility are actions viewed as more fun than productive or, because of anxiety, you rush to just do something rather than sitting still.

As an example, one morning I witnessed a man running late for his train. He dashed up the platform next to his presumed train, and began jumping up and down, waving his arms in hysterics trying to catch the attention of the train conductor. After getting no response, he ran down the platform to each compartment, madly trying to open each door so he wouldn't be left behind.

He continued this same approach down the entire length of the train. Once he reached the end, he ran back to the front of the train, trying desperately to catch the conductor's attention – again to no avail. So, he raced to the opposite side of the train, doing the same activity of trying to open each door and with a similar result.

When he finally got back to the front of the train again, he did something different. Out of breath, he walked over to the departure board and located his train. As you might expect, he was at the wrong platform and now his train was really about to leave him if he didn't hurry! As I observed the event unfold, several factors and certain assumptions informed me that this man had been wasting his time from the start.

If you don't know which train is yours, does it make sense to spend extra energy running to catch it?

Initially I noticed that the train was not running. Secondly, there were no lights on in the train, there were no passengers on the train, and there were no attendants standing on the platform at various points to assist passengers getting on and off, as would be the usual.

All of this told me that it was not likely his train. In a calm state, I had rational thinking.

However, in a state of anxiety and facing the unknown, the man's thoughts had raced to different conclusions, which at that time derailed his goal of catching his train. His *tasks of futility* were present from the start and he used additional energy on actions that took away from his goal of catching his train.

Tasks of futility often are a result of *reacting* rather than *responding* to a situation. Similar to the man and his train, you're more likely to act without thinking when you are anxious and you face an unknown.

If this man had checked the arrivals and departures board when he first arrived, he would have saved himself time and energy. In addition, he was not conscious of the signs the train was providing – for example that it wasn't running, there were no lights on, there were no passengers on the train, etc. His internal panic created a situation where he missed the obvious. Further, if he knew he was going to be late, he needed a strategy to ensure that he filtered only the information and steps which would lead to him catching his train.

This is a more reflective type of response, in which he was prepared for what he was about to encounter. A response strategy could have resembled the following: While on the way to the train station, he could have his mode of payment ready, luggage in hand, ticket and passport readily available, and know the train number.

He could recall the layout of the train station and the process to get through security or look for the nearest attendant who could help him. If this were his first time at the train station or if he couldn't recall, there was likely a departure board he could have located and his train would likely be near or at the top of the list (because it was about to leave!).

Managing actions and minimizing wasted movements when you're establishing new behaviors is no different. Thoughtful planning when you're not stressed or experiencing anxiety from the unknown enables you to think more clearly prior to engaging in an activity.

When you're in the middle of an activity, anxiety in the moment clouds your judgment about necessary actions. So, if you run into obstacles (or start chasing the train) remember that some activities provide more benefit toward achieving your desired outcome than others.

To know which activities are most productive, be thoughtful about what you're trying to achieve. The focus of your plan is on those value-added activities that enhance your ability to achieve your goal, versus those that waste your time. Through this approach, when the unforeseen does occur, you will have the energy to respond more appropriately.

By looking deeper when planning, you can minimize Tasks of Futility and the number of decisions you'll need to make while making a change.

Solution

When planning for your change, consider:
» What in your environment (people, places, or things) is influencing your ability to change behaviors?

» What can you do to establish a new relationship with your environment or new routines so you may achieve your goals?
» Where can you remove *Tasks of Futility*?

Analyze your environment and look for routines, situations, or people that may hinder your ability to do something different. While not a fail-safe, integrating strategies to manage them will help.

Plan for Noise

In addition to discomfort, there will also be noise from your internal voice or environment that may disrupt your progress.

There are certain roadblocks and noise that are appropriate. They offer signs or warnings for us to adjust our actions. The difference between those roadblocks that are noise and those that are useful depends on the situation. What you are hearing? Where is it coming from? How much weight does it carry toward what you want to achieve?

By changing your story, you are also changing the story of how it (place or thing) or they (people) experience you. Managing change in your environment can be difficult as it often means dealing with expectations that you will act and react in the same way you have in the past or in alignment with what you've inadvertently taught others to believe about you.

The animated film *Ratatouille* offers a perspective on choice and transformation that we can learn from in its lead character, a rat named Remy. Humor me as I briefly retell the tale, with some license of editing for expediency.

In spite of being a rat, Remy longed to be a chef and not to eat from the garbage. One day, he becomes separated from his group and is swept away in the sewers under Paris.

Along his travels to return to the rat colony, Remy befriends a young human – a would – be chef working in a prominent restaurant. Though hesitant to leave the restaurant and the world of cooking, Remy decides to visit the rat colony and see his father.

At a welcome home ceremony, Remy's father (Django) becomes agitated when Remy indicates he is leaving the colony permanently and going back to the restaurant. Django walks Remy outside, where he then points out dead rats hanging in a window. "*This* is the way things are. You can't change nature," Django noted.

However, Remy was unconvinced and more determined. He reminded his father that change is natural and starts when we decide. Remy then begins walking in the opposite direction of the colony, presumably back to the restaurant.

This tale reflects the choice Remy made to become the rat he wanted to be. It required acknowledgment of what he wanted, the confidence to take action,

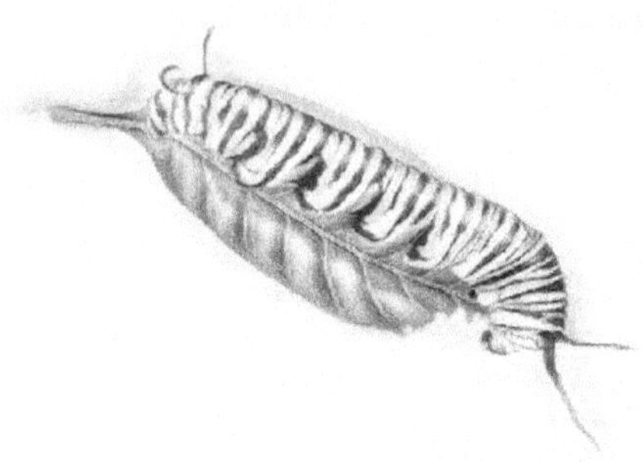

and his management of the environment around him.

Our environments offer distractions from our overall purpose and the changes we are seeking. Simply, the environment can create noise.

In our day-to-day lives, we manage to make progress despite the noise. For instance, you could be working, then, all of a sudden, a co-worker asks us a question that distracts from the immediate thought process or work goal. When transforming, the more distractions you are compelled to manage, the harder it will be to focus on new tasks. Too many distractions can lower your likelihood of success in achieving your new behaviors and goals.

Solution

To improve your story, you must change the relationships you have with your environments (that is, people, places, or things). That includes changing the way you see yourself, such as building confidence while looking for a new job. Or, it may be changing your relationship with shopping and food if you are trying to lose weight. Perhaps you need to change the relationship you have with future significant others, if past partners have derailed you from your goal of a healthy relationship. Regardless of scenario, taking intentional steps in managing your relationships with your existing environments is important during transformation.

Action:

» Be sure to consider what in the environment (person, place, or thing) will influence your ability to achieve this goal, both positively and negatively.

From the previous examples, identifying support and planning for noise could resemble:

Example 1 – Dan: To learn more about myself and become more confident in my gifts, talents, and abilities

» **Planning for Noise**
  — I need to manage through working from home and deciding not to walk each day
  — For the cooking class, I need to ensure I have created a grocery list ahead of shopping
  — Fostering more productive work relationships, I need to let go of historical feelings of several leaders so I can move forward

Example 2 – Lisa: Reduce the Feeling of Being Overwhelmed

» **Planning for Noise**
  — My internal noise - How much am I truly willing to give up to others?
  — I need to plan around staff relying on me for all decisions and strategy

PART IV SUMMARY – DIRECTION
OPERATE WITH INTENTION: PAUSE. PROCESS. REFLECT.

You're building the capability of forethought. You have realized what it takes to focus on building a plan that considers your narrative and themes that support your goal, while also considering how the environment or support system requires management. You further reviewed how to avoid tasks of futility. Remember the guy chasing the train? As the quote from author Richard Bach tells us:

"Listen to what you know instead of what you fear."

Your efforts have been to continue to listen to yourself, reducing your fear of what you don't know. Finally, you focused on your *Return on Enjoyment*.

Your journey to this point has been intentionally focused on thinking and planning. This mental exercise has been time-consuming and maybe a little frustrating. While physical progress may be minimal at this point, rest assured, you *have* made progress. These steps have established the foundation for achieving your target.

To move forward, you are now being asked to plan around six steps:

1. Based on the narrative you're transforming, what is your priority?

2. What are you willing and *not* willing to do?
    a.   This is about your choice, so how might your choices influence your ability to achieve your goal?
    b.   What unintentional consequences may result from what you're not willing to do that will impact your story?

3. How are you operating with intent to achieve your priority?
    a.   Be sure to consider what in the environment (person, place, or thing) will influence your ability to achieve this goal, both positively and negatively.
    b.   Will your capabilities meet what you perceive your environment to be in the future?
    c.   What are unavoidable activities or realities in your life that you'll need to continuously monitor to avoid setbacks?

4. How will you measure the consistency of your behaviors over time?
    a.   What does or would success look and feel like?
    b.   What is your reward for a sense of accomplishment?

5. Where might you need support (either to build a skill or hold you account-able) to help you transform?

6. What is your Return on Enjoyment?
    a.   When during the transformational process are you going to give your-self a break and NOT think about doing something new/different?
Like a caterpillar, you are exploring a new direction.

Be mindful of where you need support, becoming sidetracked with tasks of futility (like the man running after the train), or by trying to do too much all at once (reducing your decision points).

As with all plans, yours will be mired in imperfection and reveal surprises that cannot be addressed until you put it into action. Plans are intended to be flexible, and through regular assessment of your progress, they can be modi-fied throughout your journey.

You've now built the foundation toward experiencing your transformation, with P.A.C.E.

Part V

EXPERIENCE

TRANSFORMATION REALIZED

*"For we pay a price for everything we get or take in this world;
and although ambitions are well worth having, they are not cheaply won."*
— Lucy Maud Montgomery

ALL STORIES ARE TOLD FROM what someone did, not what was planned and didn't do. This is your time to actualize transforming your story.

You've been setting small intentions throughout this book. *Discovery* brought clarity and priority of what you are solving. The *Principle of You* focused on the interpersonal exploration of who you are, previous choices, and how you've built a framework of people and places that support you. Your *Plan* consolidated each area and factored in specific steps to consider for becoming something else… Someone more.

Your intention now is to build the capability of self-regulation by experiencing your transformation.

Your ambition to transform comes with a cost that will never be returned: time and energy. The first step toward focused investment of your time and action is to prioritize the capabilities you want to experience in the next month and then the actions you want to take, through writing a note to your future self. This leads to establishing weekly and daily actions that will get you closer to your goal.

At the conclusion of each week, there will be time to manage your P.A.C.E., and create space to reflect on your progress, adjust actions or expectations, and re-plan as necessary.

This is not a one-size-fits-all process, but rather a framework that establishes a baseline from which to act. If you are not yet clear on the behaviors you want to see or do, commit to removing something or seek more clarification by revisiting your *Discovery* and *Plan* parts earlier.

Step 1: Write a Note to Your Future Self

From your *Plan*, consider your future you and your environment one month from now. Write a letter to your future self through the lens of having achieved your transformation. What would you say to yourself? What are you doing? How would you describe the way you feel? What are your new routines? What is new in your environment? Where are you continuing to build capabilities or where would you believe you might still be struggling?

This exercise requires that you to get clear on the actions you should take to realize your transformation. When you are done with your letter, put it in an envelope, seal it inside, and sign the envelope with the date a month from now. Store the letter somewhere where you can find it.

Step 2: Actions for Transformation

From this letter and aligned to your two to three behaviors to achieve your transformation, ask yourself – what can you start this week?

Start by identifying situations that can be leveraged or changed so you are integrating your desired behaviors into existing routines. This will reduce the chances of talking yourself out of doing what you promised you would do.

Also, don't mistake what you want with what you need to meet your goal. You want to have a job, but don't mistake that for a career if the job doesn't align to your priority. Identify where and how you will apply your prioritized actions (starting today) over the coming weeks by reorganizing your routines and filling each week with meaning.

Consider the following:
» What activities or routines during the week will you integrate into your desired actions?
» What routines must you intentionally manage, alter, or stop that will impact your desired actions?
» What NEW routines should you create or will reinforce your desired behaviors?
» Where might you need support?
» When during the week are you going to give yourself a break and NOT think about doing something new/different?

Based on what you decided was most important, every day should reflect actions that get you closer to your transformation. That said, life is intertwined with activities that offer little room for negotiation that will conflict with your changes.

Making dinner for the kids. Going to work. Keeping commitments to our local county board. Food shopping for the family. While each is important, they offer reasons for not taking action in areas where you want to change. Further, there will be days when you won't have the time, energy, or interest to work your plan.

When identifying actions to take, keep in mind:

» **Known Actions** – What are those actions you know you should be doing, but have not taken?
» **Need for Support** – What support do you need to build your internal capability to ensure you stay on track? (e.g. Do you need a gym membership, or a personal trainer? Would working out with someone else help motivate you to stay on track? Do you need to reach out to friends or mentors to stay centered on your goal?)
» **Thinking of Your Environment** – What in your environment will you need to manage? (e.g. your friends, not knowing how to cook so you eat restaurant food all time, or working late so you lack time to reinforce healthier eating habits.)
» **Your Routines** – What situations do you need to regularly monitor that could keep you where you are? (e.g. creating a new grocery list prior to shopping, leaving for work 15 minutes earlier, creating daily to-do lists, etc.)
» **What Are You Choosing?** – Based on what you are willing and un-willing to do, how do your desired behaviors match with your future wants and needs? (You may feel the changes you are making are too drastic all at once, or you may want to eat with fewer restrictions during special occasions.)
» **Timing** – To prevent yourself from feeling overwhelmed, set only one or a few actions that you are committed to accomplishing this week.

Again, manage your P.A.C.E. You do not have to accomplish all of the actions in your *Plan* at one time.

Be mindful that when you start taking action, you will unconsciously look for social cues and reactions from the past to verify you are on track. Your transformation may offer new reactions that you are not accustomed to, which is ok. Continue to trust yourself as you move forward.

BARTENDING TIPS TO CONSIDER

The "cheap mistake" and the ability to "consolidate your movements" are two points I learned in Bartending School.

Specific to the *cheap mistake,* our instructor noted that when making a drink requiring only a liquor and juice, the bartender should pour the juice first. The reason? If you over-pour the juice, it's "cheaper" to toss out the juice and start the drink over versus the cost of over-pouring liquor (which is more expensive to replace) and having to pour it out.

As a patron, over-pour of liquor can be seen as a good thing, whereas it has a cost component for the business. Aligned to your weekly plan, incorporate time to make the cheap mistakes, where if you fail (or over-pour) it happens in situations that are not as costly.

As you are looking to build your capabilities to transform, the idea is to use this time for doing, refining, and building. These situations allow you to test new behaviors in a safe environment.

Avoid wasted resources and energy by thinking like a bartender.

Secondly, *consolidate your movements.* You can do this by taking purposeful action by eliminating or minimizing unnecessary steps. In the bartending context, the focus was removing wasted steps that would impact efficiency and responsiveness. Specific to a scenario of making several drinks at one time, your movements are consolidated by knowing the ingredients in each drink, where your tools are located, and the liquor placement behind the bar.

When combining my drink knowledge and the bar set-up, I was more efficient when it came to making drinks. This, in turn, sped up my process for moving from one customer to another – and that ultimately led to more money.

Applying these techniques with your intention, look for opportunities during the week (i.e. your bar set-up) where knowing your *Plan* (i.e. the drink recipe) you can incorporate behaviors into current routines or situations (i.e. making the drink) – all of which help bring you closer to achieving your transformative goal.

The consequences of not consolidating your movements are becoming overwhelmed and wasting time. I'm asking you to emphasize those new behaviors that have the most impact. This will minimize the amount of noise associated with old habits. Further, identify opportunities to remove routines that negate or work against what you are trying to achieve.

Several years ago, I met a gentleman at the airport who was in construction. As we were discussing our careers, he began to describe a situation at a local university that encapsulated the idea of making a cheaper mistake.

In his story, he described how the university was expanding the campus by adding several new buildings. After building one particular structure, they incorporated adjacent parking lots, sodded grass, and then provided only a few sidewalks to enter the building. Then they waited.

Over a semester, they allowed students to access the building by the few sidewalks leading to the building or through the grass.

The engineers knew the students would walk to the building's entrances to the building using the most efficient route. Thus, after a semester, these engineers created additional paths in the grass in the areas where the grass was most worn.

This allowed students to follow the same paths they had created previously, while also preserving the grass areas by eliminating the creation of unnecessary walkways. What began as a cheaper mistake than placing sidewalks students didn't use delivered additional benefits by way of consolidating movements. Engineers were able to save time in planning and money by laying paths that had demonstrated value in meeting students' needs as opposed to those that may have only served an aesthetic purpose.

Recall Lisa who felt overwhelmed and was operating with intent by delegation. She decided to use currently scheduled promotional events and meetings as opportunities for her staff to take a lead and provide her with an update. Yet in the Dan in the first example, to meet his goal of fostering more productive relationships, actually cancelled meetings and used the time to build an engagement strategy.

Managing your transformation allows you to maximize your energy.

REDUCE YOUR DECISION POINTS

"I don't want them to think."

That's the response a colleague and I received from the VP of HR when building an employee survey for her management team. Her rationale? She feared that questions that made them think would cause the managers not to fill out the survey.

While we appreciated her sentiment, the questions were developed to gather their opinions – which naturally would require them to think.

As time has passed, I can understand her perspective (albeit misguided and limited) and the drain that occurs with nonstop thought going on before and during changes. The concern isn't about having a decision to make or in thinking, but rather reducing the weight of numerous conscious decisions you face when doing something new.

When it comes to behavior change, your conscious thinking about your plans, actions, and how to navigate your environment is taxing. The more times a day you have to consciously consider the right decision, the more likely you are to make the wrong choice.

What research has shown in this regard is that: (1) the more times you have to make a decision contrary to your normal behaviors, the more likely you will make the wrong decision for that behavior; or (2) you will acquiesce on other decisions because you are tired. When you are tired, you just react with the action that comes naturally rather than the behaviors that will lead to your change.

Take an example of parents teaching their children to clean their room. They might remind their children continuously, but to do that every day is draining. In frustration, the parents may sit back and give up, thinking, "Let their room be dirty." The everyday reminders aren't worth it."

Solution

When you are changing your routines and behaviors, you are consciously and continuously thinking about the change. Successful behavior changes I've experienced and observed reduced the number of decisions made by doing the following:

» **Plan Ahead** – Planning for situations where the behavior change would occur and minimizing the number of situations and instances when they had to *consciously* think about doing the right thing.
» **Set Realistic Expectations** – Behavior change, even when planned for, is hard to follow through on every day at first. Individuals successful with change were *consistent* in their behavior and did not beat themselves up when they were not. They refocused for the next opportunity.
» **Support** – When a decision needed to be made, those who were successful had a support system to reinforce and support the right (or desired) decision. Surrounding yourself with a support system for your goals creates an environment where success is more likely to occur.

NEW BEGINNINGS: YOUR INTENTION

> *"Be the person you are, not the person people see you as."*
>
> **— Dr. B.**

New beginnings can bring about unease. Acting on your transformation opens you up to relaxing your defenses and redefines how you view yourself. This can be very exciting, very confusing, or both.

Remember, even if you take action, it doesn't mean you will get what you want. You may have to explore multiple actions before finding one that proves successful. But, if you don't do anything, you'll be guaranteed to not achieve your goal.

Trust that you know yourself. Trust that you have a plan, one that is flexible enough to evolve based on what you know and what you don't. Trusting in this foundation allows you to start building your capabilities.

While I was coaching one man, he expressed a desire to change roles, but had a fear of what was next. Reviewing previous roles, he described starting in a tactical distribution job then steadily progressing into additional positions within that same department, with little knowledge of the roles and without having a college degree.

His movement through the organization was built on trust from others, and hard work. He was speaking to me about a recent offer to move into a leadership role in a different department, where he knew no one and would be interacting with a higher level of leaders. He expressed a lack of confidence in how he'd match against these leaders, their knowledge of the organization, and their backgrounds, as they had extended degrees while he had none.

The idea of the new role was enticing. Yet, his lack of confidence in learning a new role and working with unfamiliar people didn't allow him to move past the moment. As a result, he didn't take the job.

Moving forward requires trust in your *Plan* and confidence in yourself. You'll need trust that you have planned correctly, that your survival instincts from previous experience will shine so you may avoid unnecessary trouble, and in your support system to get through the transition.

As you make decisions to take action today, you can also make a decision to do something different tomorrow.

WAKE UP AND ATTACK YOUR PLAN – THE POSSIBILITY OF 24

- » There are 24 hours in a day to realize our possibilities.
- » Every day offers a choice to use the day however we desire.
- » Possibilities exist to create, amend, and evolve.
- » Possibility is not granted to those who sit still. It's based on taking action on your priorities.
- » Wake up with intention to realize the story you want!

IDEA OF "ME": WE LIVE PARALLEL LIVES ON PAPER

"The trouble with the average person is that he does not sufficiently trust himself to create and deliver ideas."

— Norman Vincent Peale

Our stories make us real. On paper, our stories are two dimensional, a comparison of who we want to be versus who we are.

Such parallel lives are prevalent during changes. I recall working with Stacy who, as part of a broader coaching experience, wanted to end a relationship with a married man. Over several meetings, Stacy and I developed an action plan to end the relationship. The plan included the location where she would end the relationship, outlined the talking points to hit during the conversation, and discussed potential scenarios of how he might react.

In addition, it was important that she and I discuss the reason for her change, its emotional impact, and steps for her to move forward. Stacy took ownership in both starting and now ending the relationship. After several weeks, she felt ready to have the discussion with the married man.

The day they were to meet, she reiterated to me that she cared for this gentleman, but knew moving on was necessary for her story. Following their scheduled time to meet, I called Stacy to see how the conversation went and how she was doing but her phone went to voicemail.

The following morning, I sent her an email, but I did not receive a response. I decided to let a few days pass prior to contacting her again, believing that the emotional toll of the conversation and her decision may still be weighing on her. As the weeks, months, and years passed, I hoped nothing bad happened to her and that she was happy.

This story highlights the challenges of owning choices then holding one's self accountable to take action. What feels right during a time of calm preparation can be defeated by anxiety or self-defeating thoughts when it is time to act.

Choices to act or not act will either support or work against your goal.

RECOGNIZE THE MOMENT: "SPEAKING INTO THE MICROPHONE"

You can't plan for everything. Even with plans, you can get caught in the moment where emotion takes over and you're not thinking anymore, you're reacting. When you get stressed, you may return to what feels comfortable and your natural instincts.

These moments are obstacles, intended to weed out those who are not committed to their changes. All transformations always offer obstacles.

Take the couple that wants to communicate better, but during fights they revert to old communication habits that are unhealthy. She responds in a very antagonistic way in moments of stress, because that's her model. For him, during these moments, he hangs onto each word and takes what's said about him and to him very personally. That model is based on how he grew up and what was expected.

In these moments, it's similar to locomotives that already have momentum. It takes time and distance to ensure that the train slows down and eventually stops. Your behaviors are no different. When the days are calm, we give thought to what we should do. But daily moments bring about hidden or unknown aspects that may have been dormant when we were calmly planning.

When you are starting new behaviors, like a locomotive that is just starting, your wheels turn slowly without much movement. Once "the wheels" catch, you (the train) begin to move more quickly.

I recall recording my initial audiobook. My priority was to write a book for print publication, but just as important was using a medium which would allow me to share my thoughts readily.

This was the first time I had recorded anything in a studio. It was the first time I had shared my book with anyone outside of my editor. I practiced reading the book out loud. Yet nothing could have prepared me for the actual experience.

I nestled into the recording chair, put my headphones on, placed my notes on the stand in front of me, and saw the neon *recording* light flashing above the door. All I could feel was my heart pounding and self-defeating thoughts already percolating in my mind.

When I started reading, my voice was monotone, my speech was slurred, and I was speed-reading through the content.

Through the headset, the producer was offering direction. "Ian, go back to line 45 and re-read the paragraph. And remember to slow down your pace." His reminder was similar to his previous five and I was still on page 3 of 80.

While I always responded with a half-hearted "Will do," I was really thinking, "This sucks."

Over the following six hours, I was receiving real-time feedback: "Slow down," "Go back," "Enunciate your words," "Repeat that again," "Keep your pace," "Let's do it again…"

The longer I went, the more errors I made, the more effort it took to keep my energy up, keep my tone, and enunciate words. I was mentally drained and felt defeated.

As we were wrapping up for the day, the production coordinator asked how I was doing and I simply replied, "I will never do this again." Despite the production crew's positive feedback, coaching, and affable demeanor, I did not feel good about the experience.

On my way home, I found a quiet place on the beach and I just sat…reflecting on the day…taking in my thoughts.

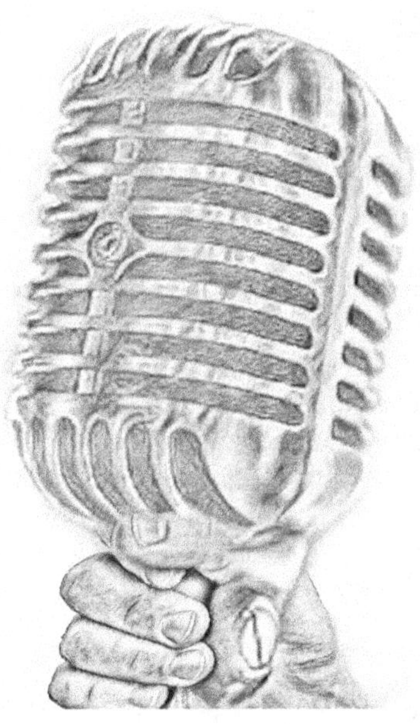

There is a victory in simply stepping up to the microphone. Even failed efforts are better than efforts never attempted.

Thoughts of personal judgment, self-doubt, and personal ridicule poured into my mind, as if staring at the water allowed me to open a levy of defeat that I felt while in the studio. That quiet moment alone also offered me the chance to acknowledge the positives. I did speak into the microphone. I was recording my book, which demonstrated a level of completion. And, I was learning how I would apply it the next day.

I was not in search for feedback for myself, but I found it empowering to acknowledge my own emotion in the moment where I had a choice to take action. This story first reflects the vulnerably associated with taking action and doing something different.

Your awareness of being in the moment when you're taking action builds your capability to manage difficult outcomes. Moments offer checkpoints for you to evaluate whether you are becoming more or less united with the transition you planned. Secondly, it demonstrates how being conscious of the moment, learning from each new experience, dealing with challenges of perceived success, then getting past those challenges will allow you to continue.

When pushing boundaries, the emotional and physical toll of the moment cannot be planned. Part of uniting your priorities with your actions is in managing internal conflict that comes from each moment. How well you manage those moments, and learn from them, may define how successful your transformation will become.

Suggestions for Experiencing the Moment

Experiencing the moment requires that you be present to your actions, surroundings, and emotions. When you sense that there is something off, consider the following:

» Recognize something is off and then pause.
» Acknowledge the emotion or behavior.
» Focus on cues about what might be contributing to the emotion or behavior.
» Acknowledge what you have done that contributes to that struggle, so you can manage actions moving forward.
» Focus on what you are willing to do in the moment or immediate future to be more effective.

My moment of challenge was only speaking into a microphone. Your intention is to understand your "microphone" and how to manage that moment.

<u>FIND BALANCE</u>

There is a balance between getting things done and doing just enough to get by.

Sometimes, energy and time do not allow you to move forward as far as you planned. These are moments to put forth an amount of effort you can successfully manage so you don't revert to derailing behaviors.

If you find yourself there, focus on the quality of your actions, not quantity (or amount of times you did it).

» **Quality** – What happens when you start speaks to effectiveness and doing it right. Establishing form.
» **Quantity** – What you build over time through repetition and finding new situations and opportunities to test your new you.

Transforming your story started from a strategic lens, establishing *Direction*, *Principles of You*, and building your *Plan*. Each phase offering context to take steps, without the psychological and emotional pull of experience. Remember, *"we all live parallel lives on paper."* This is your inflection point to take action.

Your intention is to take the next step in actualizing your story by building personal regulation through each moment of action. As author Lucy Maud Montgomery noted:

> *"For we pay a price for everything we get or take in this world; and although ambitions are well worth having, they are not cheaply won."*

You started by wring a letter to your future self, forecasting where you would be in this future, identifying scenarios to test new capabilities, and where you needed to manage your environment.

You sought instances where, similar to bartending, you could *"make the cheap mistakes"* to lower the risk of testing your actions in certain environments. Further, you *"consolidated your movements"* to avoid wasting time and to minimize the number of decisions you needed to make in the moment.

As a reminder, here is what you should have accomplished:

WRITE A NOTE TO YOUR FUTURE SELF

As covered, envision how you would like the next month to go. Setting clear and specific capabilities you want to enact and the steps to implement. On paper, write your future letter to yourself, put it in an envelope, seal it and sign the envelope with the date a month from now. Store it somewhere where you can find it.

ACTIONS FOR TRANSFORMATION

Again, your aim should be to identify where and how you will apply your prioritized actions over the <u>next week</u> by reorganizing your routines. During which activities or routines this the week will you integrate your desired actions? Consider the following:

1. What routines must you intentionally manage, alter, or stop that will impact your desired actions?

2. What NEW routines should you create or will reinforce your desired behaviors?

3. Where might you need support?

4. When during the week are you going to give yourself a break and NOT think about doing something new/different?

Anchor on your new direction. Remember that the speed with which change happens is less important than the results of those changes lasting.

You will strengthen your capabilities the more moments you test your will over the course of a day, week, and month. There may be feelings and circumstances that create inspiration, or others that create anxiety. What you thought you knew previously may now be irrelevant, much like how I felt during my studio recording.

Don't get consumed in this alteration, as experience is meant to help you find clarity that didn't exist before. As a result, you may encounter alternate methods towards achieving your transformation that you hadn't considered. If you find yourself in a place of discomfort in the moment, do not be afraid to pause, focus on what is contributing to the emotion, and readjust in the moment or immediate future to be more effective.

See each moment as an opportunity to move past linear thinking and let your mind and actions go toward your expectations.

Taking action is intended to make you less attached to the person you are and how you currently define yourself. This is a time to remind yourself that each step connects you to something bigger.
Create your possibility. You are experiencing the pages of your transformation through action, so make it one hell of a story!

You are making progress. Continue to enjoy the experience of your new capabilities with P.A.C.E.

Part VI

ATTUNEMENT

REFLECTION

"For darkness restores, what light cannot repair."
— Joseph Brodsky

YOU ARE CONSTANTLY LEARNING, WHETHER experiencing something new, being reminded of a part of yourself that you previously developed or having to alter past thoughts and habits.

Learning offers moments to acknowledge things you didn't want to happen, but must accept. These are experiences that you could not have planned, or you may even have wanted to avoid, but needed to go through nevertheless so that you could learn. It could be about actions that failed to meet with your expectations, or it might be about portions of your environment you feel you can't live without, but have to let go. If you are not learning from your experiences, you *will* revert to habits of the past.

You're building the capability of self-reflection to expand your perspective and become attuned with your actions and emotions.

If you were not clear about your intention, you may feel disappointment in these moments. Be mindful of self-judgment during reflection. Self-judgments can derail your progress and be defeatist. If you started, in part or whole, your efforts, reflecting on the past successes can be exciting. If you are not on track or if you haven't had success, you may feel stress or disappointment that you haven't moved forward. If you have these feelings, this time may inspire you to do something different.

In any case, moments offer a referendum on your choices and what you've prioritized. You may regret certain decisions or you may have ignored opportunities to take action. You have a choice as to whether such a referendum is a place of *residence* (i.e. a moment that is an indication of who you are and you're not changing) or *reference* (i.e. a moment that offers a decision point from which to move from and take action).

As you proceed from here, you may rationalize decisions in the moment to not do what you said with a well-intended (but often a misplaced promise) that you'll do it later. Further, new circumstances may cause you to struggle to consistently achieve your actions. As explained previously, situations offer resistance in order to keep you where you in the same place. This struggle forces you to live a "parallel life," one you live out versus the one put on paper. Plans on paper are free of the failure, energy, ridicule, and uneasiness that come with engaging in new behaviors and getting feedback from your environment.

You may find that frustration and stress come when you resist being yourself or experience an imbalance between your expectations versus what you achieved.

Your transformation is asking you to fight conformity and live to new expectations. We can also go overboard in criticism of ourselves if we haven't set limits or consequences that are consistent with the choices we've made. Imbalance between how you've defined success versus the results you've achieved may cause frustration. Thus, once you start "doing," you'll be in a continuous learning cycle, offering multiple touchpoints for intentional reflection.

WHAT IS YOUR PATTERN?

Hindsight offers patterns to learn or unlearn. This continuous discovery process refocuses you toward what is most important and trains you to recognize the behavioral signs that led to a result. This is the time to observe and gather information as you look to possibly reset. Further, this is a good time to let go of what you thought you knew about your transformation which no longer holds value – including your ideas, expectations, and past experiences. Your patterns will come from two areas: *you* and *your environment*.

You

When you reflect, you're considering how well you have lived your priorities. If you continuously prioritize derailing behaviors over those new habits to transform, then there may be routines to address. What have your characters and choices done that either helped or hindered you in moving forward?

It's similar to my colleague who wanted to lose weight. However, her pattern was to wake up in the middle of the night and drink several glasses of milk. Such a pattern was not helpful in achieving her goal.

Reflect on the Principles of You and how your history is showing up each day in positive or negative ways.

<u>*Your Environment*</u>

Your environment will also reflect a portion of what you achieved, your insecurities, and strengths.

As an example, I suggested Monica update, then upload her resume to several prominent job sites for visibility, and then wait. While I believed she updated her resume to the extent she could, we needed feedback.

Such feedback would not come in an interview, but from the types of roles recruiters would offer her based on what she included in her resume.

After a month, Monica and I reviewed the feedback. Recruiters were reaching out to her for certain roles, so we compared that against what she wanted. If she was not receiving the types of roles that reflected her skill or the interest expressed in her resume, then she would likely not receive the jobs she wanted.

In this situation, Monica was telling her story (through actions) in her resume and the environment was offering feedback.

There are times when you will need to do something different to receive the feedback you want (in Monica's case editing and clarifying key points within her resume to receive the roles she wanted). Other times your actions will already align with your desires. When you are testing capabilities, find ways to identify feedback within your environment that offers perspective on what you are trying to achieve.

If you have missed an opportunity to take action, use this time to inspire yourself to take a new approach. You must remove or minimize self-criticism that could keep you from moving forward. Focus more interest in the reasons why you are not taking action (similar to your exploration in *Discovery*), and less interest in the fact that you didn't achieve an end result. This reflection will help you determine where you are getting stuck.

Reflection is an ongoing process, where you are interpreting, creating, changing, and perpetuating beliefs about yourself.

During this time, you may realize that what you committed to previously (sometimes months and years ago) is no longer the path you should be taking. Be careful not to shut down. Repurpose your energy in a new direction.

OH, THAT'S NOT GOOD

"If you are not embarrassed by your first version of your product, you've launched too late."

— Reid Hoffman

Daily reflection can be draining. You can get caught up trying to catch up on what you didn't do. Or, you might become overly critical from a lack of action. As you gain clarity on what you are responding to, objective reflection will occur either in the moment or shortly after the situations in which your behaviors were experienced. That reflects progress.

Oh, that's not good!

Three months had passed since my audiobook recording, and those were my initial thoughts after listening to the first edited version. All of the fears and thoughts I identified earlier while recording my audiobook (in the moment) were captured in infinity and were now being conjured up in my mind. All of the points I had been coached on and felt in the moment (I was monotone, my tone was up and down, my speech slurred) came out.

Even as I listened, I realized that the content I was reading was missing key points I was trying to make! It took me three weeks, listening in pain-staking detail to an incoherent monologue, to assess the effort. The recording acted as a time capsule of experience and emotion. What is usually lost in the memory of time was now a frozen reminder.

Sometimes you do not realize where your efforts will lead when you begin. In those instances, wait for the paint to dry and work your way out of your corner.

When I was finally finished writing all of my feedback, three things came to mind: (1) no wonder it took the producers three months to edit the recording; (2) thank goodness they were the only ones to have heard it; and (3) I needed to start from scratch.

May I have been overly critical of myself? Possibly. But I knew I would not be satisfied with releasing content to others that could be better.

Listening to my voice and hearing my words provided a mirror of clarity of what I had been fighting through in my characters, my environment, what I wanted to change. It was an astonishing experience.

Upon reflection, I laughed at myself knowing I was exactly where I needed to be based on my transformation cycle. I used that version and the related reflection as a place for *reference* to acknowledge: (1) that regardless of my critique, I had completed the recording of the audiobook; and (2) there were specific areas I believed needed refinement, and I could build on by this recording again.

While you may not have a recording to analyze your progress, what you will have is your reflection of some outcome. It's ok to be embarrassed.

EXPERIENCES EVOLVE

You may find that you've honed the behaviors that are in your plan. Part of your reflection may require that you expand the arenas for applying your new behaviors.

Do you have time to talk?

That infamous six-word phrase always makes our ears perk up with interest, concern, and surprise every time it's directed towards us in conversation. On this day, it was a text I received from John who needed to vent.

He was in the midst of transforming how he experienced relationships. Having recently divorced and re-entering the world of dating, his goal was to be in a healthy relationship of honest dialogue, especially during hard conversations. Plus, he wanted to clarify his wants from the start of a relationship.

When we finally connected, the first words I heard were *Ahhhhhhhh, I just need to get this off my chest.*

John described his current relationship and how things were going well until a recent conversation. It started when he was taking more control in the relationship, and she was not comfortable with some of the things he was doing. This came to a boiling point ahead of a date where she expressed her concerns. John then blew it off until after they returned from their excursion. At the end of the date, he began to say his good-bye, and she brought up her concerns again. Instead of having the conversation and listening, he said "I guess this is it and I will talk to you later."

As we talked, John recognized that he could handle hard conversations when *ending* a relationship. However, he was frustrated that he had not progressed to the point where he could handle hard conversations while still being *in* the relationship.

John's experience hasn't altered his desire to be in a healthy relationship nor the progress he made. It only changed the circumstances in which his actions would be happening and how far he was pushing himself to evolve. Transformations see progress in the form of better or different questions, which in turn drives evolution.

For the Lisa described earlier, who was struggling with the overwhelmed/retired balance, she was good at delegating small activities, and establishing her personal time so she *felt* retired. Her ability was stretched when she was asked to delegate bigger activities given her need for control, which invariably cut into her personal time.

Your experiences should evolve, and as you do, your abilities will be tested. What you thought you did well in one arena may not apply to other areas. If you're not testing your abilities, it may be the result of feeling comfortable in your current place, a lack of interest in moving forward, fear, or simply not knowing what to do.

That evening, John sent me an email based on what he took away from our conversation. The last paragraph acknowledged self-reflection and a perseverance that you should keep in mind:

> *"I am proud of my growth the last two months.*
> *I accept my decisions as the best I could do in the moment and will always*
> *put myself out there and just do. Try, fail, get up, and repeat."*

Continue your transformative path.

I'M GOING TO NEED YOU TO DO BETTER

If you have not done what you set out to do, use your feelings and time to inspire yourself to do something different this week, this month.

Notice where you misaligned with progress by escaping or avoiding what you had planned.

There will be times when you will lie to yourself during the transition. You'll rationalize the reasons you've taken certain actions and justify where you are. In those moments, I'm going to need you to do better. *You're* going to need you to do better.

We mostly attribute the need to do better to others. They have toilet paper on their shoe, they didn't replace the ink cartridge in the printer, their dog pooped on your lawn, and your favorite team didn't draft the right players. We witness all of these with the thought of "I'm going to need you to do better." As we assign such judgments to others, we must also assign such judgment to ourselves.

Self-reflection offers time to assess actions we know we *should have* done but didn't. I should have stayed on the treadmill 10 minutes longer, but I wanted to save some energy. I'm not going to discuss this challenge with my boss today, I will wait until our next one-on-one, etc., etc.

There is a tendency to rationalize what we should do. However, this is about effort. Did you give it your all? Did you set yourself up for success? If not, do better. When living in the moment, there is no postponing action to another time. Ironically, most transformations start with what one *should* already be doing, but has delayed.

There is a phrase in the practice of yoga that says, "When a pose becomes difficult is when the pose truly begins." It is the same with evaluating your actions, or lack thereof. Acknowledging *should do* versus what you *are doing* is exercising personal accountability regarding effort.

COMMITMENT: BUG/WINDSHIELD

> *"There are moments of darkness, that eclipse us to blackness;*
> *but when your purpose is clear, those are the good days."*
> **—Unknown**

Let's put reflection into context. You'll experience the ebb and flow of when you're executing your *Plan* versus realizing that you haven't done all that you could. You are living your "parallel life."

Transformations offer a trade-off between action and energy – inclusive of the emotion of the moment – that can't be addressed by planning. Fatigue and external resistance force us back into old habits. Know that successes and failures are part of your transformation cycle.

This cycle can be described through a story of a bug and a windshield. Imagine for a moment, you're driving and a bug hits your windshield. The bug had its destination, as did the car's windshield. Applied to transformations, there'll be days when you're the "bug" – where you'll be stopped without warning. Moments when it's a struggle to accomplish what you planned, whether it is your fault or caused by something or someone else. Conversely, there are moments when you are the "windshield." Where you are acting on your plan and have a sense of accomplishment and progress.

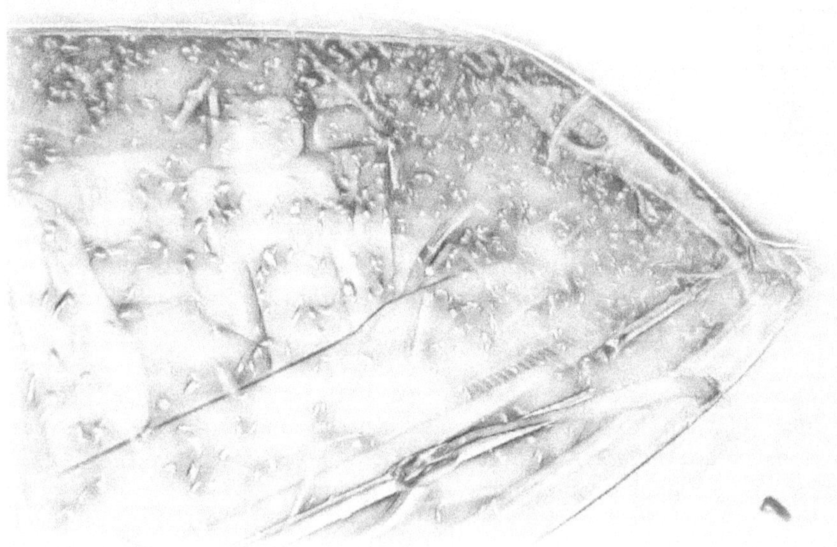

Some days you're the bug. Other days you're the windshield.

It's unrealistic to believe you'll always be the bug or always be the windshield. Being the windshield builds self-confidence to sustain your actions. Your place as the bug offers an opportunity to learn from what actions aren't working, adjusting your behaviors to those that may work in the future, and then trying again. This continuum offers an opportunity to be vulnerable and to continuously build your capabilities.

As noted, such cycles also impact self-confidence. A study by Lindsley, Brass, and Thomas identified three cycles that emerge when looking at confidence and performance: a self-correcting cycle, an upward spiral, or downward spiral.

Self-correcting spirals occur when you analyze your performance and make adjustments in future efforts to achieve your goals. From these adjustments, you may experience an upward spiral as well as overconfidence as continuous success decreases the levels of experimentation necessary to learn. Conversely, downward spirals create self-doubt.

You have made yourself vulnerable to do something new. At times it will bring success, other times failure. Maintaining a positive perspective, while adjusting, remaining consistent, or both, will enable a path toward sustaining your capabilities. Be careful about the information you use for reflection so you do not lose the will to experiment or the confidence to move forward.

The more comfortable you get with transformations and your capabilities, the easier it will be to embrace the cycles that come along with transformations – instead of being overwhelmed by them.

With continued effort, reflection, and adjustment, you'll become the windshield more frequently. Just know, being the bug is an equally essential part of building your ongoing capability to transform.

EQUAL EFFORT IS NOT ALWAYS REQUIRED

You can put in all the effort you had in the moment, come up with the best *Plan* with the information you had, and still not be successful.

There are actions within your transformation that are "just do its." Those that do not require much thought or energy. They are of the "I am calling a health care professional to get my annual physical" variety. Then you receive your physical.

However, there are others that require both emotional and physical energy that push you past comfort. They take the form of "Now that I am going to the gym, there are other people around who will see me, my size, or my struggle with the lightest of weights. That makes me uncomfortable."

Both present steps toward transforming, but they are unique in the type effort and emotions brought out.

Effort and plans can be refined, as your energy may not match the planned effort and behavior you want.

You will not attack your plan with the same energy and focus every day. Those who consistently focus on their new behaviors and learnings are more likely to reach their capabilities faster than others. But just like any race, there are days when your focus and energy will be better than others.

Thus, when reflecting on progress, consider how your effort and emotions varied based on the tasks you completed or did not.

CHANGE FOR THE SAKE OF CHANGING

"The only difference between perseverance and stubbornness is your willingness to listen to feedback and do something different in hard times."
—Dr. B.

Research has demonstrated that the quality of your planning is overridden by constant changes in goals. Changing your plans can be effective but ensure that you're not changing the plan just for the sake of changing it or because you're avoiding actions that are hard.

I overheard a woman, when asked if her diet was working, respond: "It works if you do it right, but no one does it right!" Aside from assuming from her response that her diet wasn't working and finding her honesty refreshing, I wondered what caused her plan not to work.

Did she get to a certain point of her diet and chose not to move forward at the first sign of challenge or wasn't experiencing results fast enough?

She may have given up too quickly on her plan. Quick success is a difficult proposition because hardly anyone executes their changed behaviors right initially.

It's like watching Looney Tunes' old cartoon characters Wile E. Coyote and the Roadrunner. For those too young to have watched or too old to remember, the cartoon was based on the Coyote (Wile E.) hunting a fast bird (the Road Runner) in the desert, hoping to eat the bird for dinner.

The short stories followed Wile E. scheming to catch the Road Runner using various devices, but he was never successful. What made the cartoon fun was the perseverance and creativity that Wile E. demonstrated in trying to catch the Road Runner.

There was an important aspect of Wile E.'s failed efforts worth noting. After each failed attempt to catch the Road Runner, the coyote would usually build a new plan or device to catch the bird. Wile E. rarely used the same device twice.

Reflecting on the cartoon, it is interesting that Wile E. rarely gave himself the chance to learn from mistakes or hone a capability on a particular device to catch the Road Runner. He just started over.

Like Wile E., you may be experiencing this challenge. You have a goal. You built your plan with specific actions to accomplish, and when the plan doesn't work, there's an immediate impulse to throw everything away and start brand new.

You're not allowing yourself an opportunity to assess, adjust, and try again. If not quitting altogether, you may move to something you perceive will provide a quicker or better result. There is a time and place to change course, but changing too often brings about fatigue. Resist the urge to act on the immediate result and – as discussed in *Discovery* – refocus on the core actions of what may not be working and solve for them.

It must be said again, that you may realize certain activities are "tasks of futility" and should be removed or updated. Upon this realization, simply change those behaviors.

Remember, life and transformations act in stages. Each stage is a moment to build capability, reinforce direction, and ascertain a new focal point for change. These stages also offer the tension of unknown futures. Changing without learning misses an opportunity to refine new behaviors.

Ask yourself if you are rushing to act based on a sense of fear or panic. Reflection builds a capability of trusting your insights and perceptions in an authentic way. Just make sure you are aligned to what you want to transform as well as what you are willing to do.

WHAT HAPPENS IF YOU GET STUCK?

There is an ebb and flow throughout all changes. There may be instances where you're in the middle of transforming and you get stuck. Being stuck can call attention to attachments of your past that may be preventing you from evolving.

Your goals may not have changed, but perhaps you are not experiencing the same gains as when you started, or your excitement is gone. Or, you've met your original goal and now want something else.

In these situations, you can notice when old habits may be getting in the way of progress. Pay attention to what is causing you confusion, what you're fighting against, and how you or your environment are contributing to your struggle.

Solutions include:
» Have compassion for yourself. You may not be doing anything wrong. You may need more time for results to show.
» If you believe it's a mental obstacle holding you back, consider:
    — Is what you set out to do still a priority?
    — How might your historical characters and environment influence your immediate need for survival versus what you're transforming?
» If you're not getting as much return on your effort or enjoyment (i.e. you've hit a plateau or need a new perspective), consider:
    — Do you need support or someone/a group to offer accountability or a new perspective?
    — Are there parts of your routine that require altering?

My intention is to re-anchor you to your purpose, balance your expectations, and reflect on what may be derailing you or causing you to get stuck. Your intention is to re-commit to what you are building, its foundation, what you are willing to do, and adjust your *Plan* for action.

Success and failure offer signs. You didn't just arrive at either destination. Your intention is to get clear on what you see as important based on your actions, acknowledging progress and realizing your reality. You are building the capability of ongoing self-reflection and learning. If you refrain from learning and, just as importantly, applying it to future moments, *darkness will restore what light* (learning) *cannot repair.*

This reflection time is an evolution of operating with intention previously noted in other chapters. However, it focuses on using your experience to plan, rather than just introspection of words. Each moment offers you a place of reference or residence that defines how close you get to your target.

Also, this time is not meant to focus on reasoning behaviors away. Rationalizations of actions may keep you in your old "boxes" of doing. Recall, that we live parallel lives on paper. What you wrote might not reflect what you really meant. There will be times when you are the bug and not the windshield.

Give yourself permission to feel what you feel, even if you judge yourself. The key is to notice what is – and what is not – working and to transform.

While reflection can occur any time, doing so weekly fosters incremental steps toward building new habits. One week does not define expertise, but rather highlights actions that will either lead to painting yourself in a corner or lead to greener pastures. When starting something new, you will rely on ingrained actions and beliefs for stabilization. When you consider your past week:

1. What can you count as a success?

2. What habits can you build on?

3. What are you looking forward to the most and why?

4. What opportunities did you miss that you could act on in the coming week?

5. Where do you require more focus?

With that context, re-plan for your coming week:
6. What are you going to prioritize for the week?

7. Where might you need additional help or support?

8. When during the week are you going to give yourself a break and NOT think about doing something new/different?

The butterfly doesn't remember being a caterpillar, but you have the luxury of learning, so your past can serve as a springboard to your future. Learn to become something new.

MONTHLY PROGRESS

After several weeks of reflection, assessing progress and consolidating themes against your narrative is important.

Similar to your weekly reflection, the purpose of the *monthly* check-in acknowledges the choices and progress you've made. There may be themes presenting themselves which offer consistent insight into how you are progressing.

But first, find the letter you wrote to your future self-several weeks ago. As you read the letter, consider the following:

1. How were you consistent with your actions? How were you not?
    a.   Consider how you may have prioritized some activities over others and how your motivation may have changed.
    b.   When do you find you compromise your priorities the most?

2. Where did you not see or feel progress?
    a.   What contributed to you not seeing or feeling progress?
    b.   What in your environment needs more management?

Irrespective of how well the actual result mirrors the one you planned on, you are closer to getting there.

This is a time to review your month, set your goals and act intentionally. Review your actions, your characters, environment, and choices to determine what is working and what is not.

Perhaps it's a time to start something new, expand your capabilities by integrating habits more deeply into your life, removing more of what is not working for you, or getting additional support to hold you accountable. As you continue your transformation into the next month:

3. Based on your weekly reflection, what behavioral themes resonate?
   a.   Do you find you are solving for the same challenges?

4. What activities or routines during the month can you build on and integrate into your daily life to support your desired actions?

5. What actions require more time to see progress? Or is it time to expand your actions to more situations?

6. What behaviors will define your success in the next month?

Finally, write another letter to your future self (again a month out), with congratulations on your continued progress!

Your priorities do not change weekly or monthly, just the weight of them do. Continue to build consistency of your actions over time, with *intention*.

Part VII

THE GIFT

SUSTAINING CAPABILITIES

*"All changes, even the most longed for, have their melancholy,
for what we leave behind us is a part of ourselves;
we must die to one life before we can enter another."*
—Anatole France

LIKE ALL EVOLUTION, CAPABILITIES MUST be continuously built, nurtured, and sustained. Sustainable behaviors become abilities when combining actions that reinforce one another over time. Initially it's a practice of building consistent habits around your knowledge, managing the environment as well as emotions in the moment.

Your gift has been the receipt of knowledge. Because knowledge is dynamic, your focus centered on building capabilities through *Discovery*, the *Principle of You*, *Direction*, *Experience*, and *Attunement*. This continuously evolves as pursuits and the environment change. You've cultivated these capabilities to face the environment and transform it into one that reinforces who you want to be. This is the reason sustainment of capabilities is important; otherwise, the gift you just achieved will wither from lack of use.

In the Bible, the story of Lazarus (John 11:1-44) presents a story of transformation. According to the story, in what would be his last miracle prior to his own resurrection, Jesus brings Lazarus back to life after he had died four days earlier. The telling of Lazarus's story ends in his resurrection, but who was he afterwards? In the broader context of a biblical meaning to the story (proof of Jesus as the son of God), such context was less important than what subsequent theologians and historians have uncovered about Lazarus story. Research on near-death experiences shows that a person's life is often transformed afterwards – from materialistic to altruistic, or self-oriented to being more compassionate. With this in mind and while an extreme example, one can surmise that Lazarus transformed to a new person upon his resurrection.

While you're not having a near-death experience, you are living to create new patterns because of the knowledge you've gained across your reading and experience. You've become a different person, initiated through a desire to transform but now authentically managed with intention. The shock of death allowed Lazarus to center on what was important to him. He knew what he cherished at that moment and all else faded away.

Even if you revert to previous behaviors, you are not the same. You now have a reference point through choice, action, and reflection that you did not have previously. These are your memories of stories past. You have gained a new pattern to rule your life.

Constant transformation offers delicate reminders of who we are and who we want to become. Sustaining and integrating new behaviors into your life will assist you in staying ready for the next target you build.

There can be an unpleasant aspect of this because of the emotional endings that come from even "the most longed for." The experience of "dying to one life" before you can "enter another" is scary. The death you experienced in one life symbolizes a transition of boundaries and actions from the "old" to "new."

Sustainment's function is to consistently practice living to new principles, anchored by the knowledge of self, persevering, and being ready to evolve for future needs.

PRACTICING LEADS TO MOMENTS: THE 10-MINUTE RECITAL

You will practice building and refining your capabilities longer than you will care to spend developing and refining them.

As an example of friend of mine, Jack, was expressing his frustration about his son's recent violin recital. He commented that he could not believe how much time he and his son spend practicing for a ten-minute recital.

I asked, "What do you mean?"

Jack quickly jumped into explaining his son's routine leading up to the recital. "Chris has a one-hour, private one-on-one violin lessons each week. Then he has a thirty-minute practice with the school band twice a week. He also has a one-hour violin practice with a separate string orchestra each Saturday, where they have a concert twice a vear. And then I want him to practice at home twice a week for thirty-minutes in the evenings."

He continued, "It's a lot of practice. And all we get out of it is to sit through a one-hour program, where Chris is only playing a song for ten-minutes that he will never play again. It's four hours a week of practice for ten minutes, and I don't like it."

The conversation turned to how Jack viewed himself as a parent and the aspiration of many parents share of wanting to offer as much support to their children as possible, so their children have the resources to do better and be more. Despite his feelings of frustration, Jack's effort

Behind every moment of greatness are countless hours of trying, failing, learning, and improving.

wasn't misplaced. All of his son's activities could be seen in the light of a goal – to increase Chris's skills in playing the violin, with the sub-goals of his ability to read music and play with others on different instruments.

The recital was a reflection of the progress of his son's capability to play "a" song using his violin. In that moment, that ten-minute song reflected his skill to that point. The conductor or teacher identified music that reflected the skills his son should acquire, maybe even pushing him slightly beyond his skills to keep him challenged. In this way, the ten-minute performance reflected progress, which his son could build on for the next practice or recital on new music.

Your transformation cannot be seen as one moment (a recital); there will be many moments that build over time so you can transform your story (being a better violinist, for example). You are finding moments to practice your capabilities, mini-recitals to showcase your skills – each one matching where you are and allowing your growth with each new piece of "music." That is how you build capabilities and sustain your transformations.

...AND START AGAIN

He'd get up. Get through the day with prioritized action. Go to sleep. Wake up. And start all over again.

That is the story of an American football athlete, no longer able to play because of an arm injury. He was transitioning from the life of an elite athlete to one struggling to move his arm for everyday life. The mental and physical challenges offered a balance between who he once was and who he was transforming to become. He went from being a 205-pound guy, who could tackle some of the strongest men, to someone he could barely recognize. Accepting his new reality took months and many conversations.

Aside from the physical transition, he was conscious (emotionally) of showing his scars. Every day it was a hurdle for him to say, "I'm not going to cover up and I'll be my true authentic self." He had to move past what other people might think or how they might see him. What mattered was how he saw himself. For him, one of his victories occurred when he showed up wearing short sleeve shirts to the practice field to watch the team. He previously had worn long sleeves to conceal his arms' atrophy. It took baby steps to get him where he needed to be mentally.

As in this example, there isn't a linear path to feeling better, mentally or physically. Transformations take daily intention and the conviction to wake up, refocus, "...and start again."

You may have reached a "good enough" state, where you fall short of your intended target, but the dissatisfaction to sustain a behavior isn't as strong as when you started. You may accept incremental progress knowing the effort you put in, but stop short of full integration. You're not feeling as overwhelmed, you're living a "mostly" healthy lifestyle, or your "team" is feeling mildly engaged and understands your challenges. You then turn your attention to other needs that are greater sources of dissatisfaction.

For Mark, whose "dot" was to better manage his team, he felt great about the progress and steps he made to engage his team, communicate with them about expectations, and review their individual goals more frequently. While he made tangible progress, feedback from interviews I conducted with several team members came back far less glowing. The team acknowledged his progress and effort, yet he still was well below what they expected.

He was devastated by the news. Mark had made progress, but he wasn't done. We discussed how he could continue building on his actions – build-

ing his "again."
Progress sometimes subdues the compelling reason to do more, especially when the progress is self-perceived. Once the reason dies, another reason takes its place. Your target moves.

Sustainment of capabilities requires a sense of continuous dissatisfaction – that compelling reason. If you still feel a compelling reason to continue, you will continue. If you perceive your reason is gone or minimized, you will move on, even if you have not met your goal. The behaviors for sustained transformation, takes continuous practice.

Intention is a gift you give yourself, one that allows you to unlock the power of your greatest ability.

INITIALLY, IT'S PERSEVERANCE...

Sustaining transformations is as much about your capabilities as it is a test of will. Perseverance and resolve reflect our greatest ability of evolution, and this is the greatest commitment you can make to yourself.

One group of people who exemplify perseverance are those who relocate across great distances or are immigrants from one area to another. Researchers in the 1950s outlined how those from the South, who migrated to the North, Midwest, and West, tended to be more goal-oriented, persistent, and not easy to discourage. These groups typically gave up everything (something they were willing to do) to seek better lives in unknown worlds. Such findings are consistent among immigrants even today, and this has even been described as the "immigrant advantage." The is advantage is not about capability but about will. When you give up everything or have a dogged mentality to reach a goal – as migrants and immigrants typically display – you have no choice but to keep going, and persevere. You *will* find a way.

But all perseverance isn't life or death. Sometimes it shows up in the most mundane situations. When discussing "The Idea of Me" earlier, recall the story of Stacy who sought to leave the married man and never responded to my follow-up requests on how her conversation went.

Ironically, I received an email from her, six years in the making. Stacy's apology for her nonresponse, as well as an expression of perseverance in the following:

> *"I did eventually break it off with (him) over a year ago. It took several attempts and I succeeded!*
>
> *It took a few years for me to put your advice into practice. I am a person who can kick ass at work, {but} takes so much more time to effectuate in my personal life."*

Your transformation may take several attempts to take hold. Effectuating – to put into force or operation – your personal transformation can be hard. Irrespective of result, your transformation takes time.

There is a *Plan* for transformation, with a clear sense of the goal, steps to achieve it, and confidence to produce the outcome. When we initially start, progress seems easy and confidence rises. We continue to push forward, even thru slight challenges. Her story reinforced that we are not time bound by our intentions. They will always stay with us.

All transformations have an inflection point where actions and intent will be tested by personal frustration, unforeseen challenges, or even those around you. All of this designed – consciously or not – to keep you where you are. Resulting in the urge to change direction prematurely or alter your plans abruptly at the first sign of resistance.

The great acts of transformation occur in the face of challenge and uncertainty. It's exercising your resolve, your internal immigrant advantage. For most of us, such situations offer a choice to persevere or stop.

For Stacy, it may have been: *Do I want to leave this married man?* For you, it may be that the time and energy to update your resume is too much, so you think: *Do I really want a new job?* Or, maybe your schedule is too hectic, or it's hard to eat healthy, so you think: *Am I willing to delegate and am I that overwhelmed? How much weight do I really want to lose?*

There will always be issues and failures. You will increase your chances of eventual success with resolve. When you find yourself at that inflection point, persist anyway. You'll be surprised what you will continue to learn about yourself and what you're able to build.

Sometimes, it's six years in the making.

<u>TIRED</u>

Sometimes you get tired of telling the same story. You want a sense of accomplishment, to know that who you are is good enough. Thinking of change can be like a scab being pulled off a scar, only to create a fresh wound to heal.

Your focus on specific behaviors can wane when a capability is achieved, becomes outdated, or it may highlight other areas that require change. It's okay to pivot to other habits and goals. What is consistent are the capabilities learned to adjust to changing targets.

When you get tired, refocus on your Return on Enjoyment, or simply pause, knowing you've made progress.

...THEN IT'S INTEGRATION

Your will is tested each time you make a decision to do something different. The moment you acquiesce to something that goes against what you want, you'll be more drawn to reverting back to old habits. Sustainment includes the consistency of doing whatever you say you are willing and unwilling to do.

New Year's resolutions are a prime example of sustainment going awry. This is a time for most people to reset their intentions for the year. One of the most sought-after resolutions is that of being healthier, and specifically losing weight. The typical scenario includes this:

January 1, a person commits to going to the gym. So, they purchase their membership, sign up for a personal trainer or special classes, and even buy new clothes for the activity. They work out with their trainer, go to their classes, and even recruit friends to go along and help them stay accountable. They are following the trainer's instruction and purchasing new foods in order to be healthy.

During the first month, they experience steady progress. During the second month, the commitment level is mostly still high, and they continue with progress. Then life events start to happen in the middle of the third month. Confidence and early reward give them a false sense of assurance about their achievement.

During this period of wavering, justifications for skipping their routines creep into their mind. Thoughts of *It's only this one time,* or *I can have a cheat day, after all it's Valentine's Day.* Always with the promise: *I will be back on my plan starting tomorrow.*

The event passes, they are back on their plan the next day, until the next event. Another cheat day, cheat meal, followed by the commitment to start again tomorrow.

Eventually the cycle continues where there are more cheat days than workout days. They eventually lose their trainer as the package is up, and they find they're spending less and less time at the gym. Now, they've reverted back to the same habits they had prior to New Year's. With a resolution started on Day One and stopped in the first quarter of the year. I often call this experience "the gym effect."

In his book, *Why We Do What We Do,* Edward Deci acknowledged the challenge of sustaining transformations through the lens of *introjection* versus *integration.* When something is "introjected" (imagine a needle that injects serum into your veins; it goes directly into your system for your body to consume it faster), we're reacting to the expectations and experiences that are placed upon us by our environment. Instances involving introjection, while achieving short-term results, limit our ability to sustain or build upon our capabilities for sustainment.

Introjection is often experienced when solving for a presenting problem, rather than embodying actions that address foundational actions for sustainment.

Integration focuses on bringing separate and unique actions into a single place that stays with you. Simply you're building behaviors into everyday decisions and the fabric of who you are. For example, by integrating a new routine of going to the gym into your regular workday, you are creating a new schedule, and a daily rhythm. These are not necessarily activities that become comfortable.

Like all *gym effects,* quick results can provide false confidence. When viewed across the long-term, results may hide necessary future actions, and before too long you may find that you have reverted to old habits that derail your progress.

CONTINUOUSLY MANAGING YOUR ENVIRONMENT

Environments can reinforce old truths that have not yet been laid to rest, similar to our dying in one life to live another. In a different scene from the movie *Ratatouille*, Anton Ego – the Food Critic – describes the restaurant food he just ate which was made by a rat. Pondering what to write for his review, he made two astute observations. The first acknowledged that critics risk very little and thrive off negative criticism that is both fun to write and read, while others offer themselves up for judgment (in this case chefs as they present food). The second acknowledged that there are times when a critic risks something and that something is in the *defense* of the new. The new, Anton says, "needs friends."

Simply, to sustain your new actions and capabilities, you need to surround yourself with routines, people, and places that reinforce who you've become. Sustaining "new" habits requires "friends" (people, places) that reinforce who you've become.

Your environment will offer signs in either support or disdain for your new direction. So, who are your "new" friends?

FINALLY... STAY READY

Many transformations are initiated from a place that is brand new. There are times where that should be the case. However, with a focus on building capabilities, you're continuously developing skills that could be transferable. This book and your experience established a foundation of capabilities that you'll want to sustain.

As you may have experienced, some actions and capabilities you tapped into may have already been started previously. The length of your "runway" to achieve something new will be correlated to where you start and the capabilities you still need to create.

It is important to continue to refine and build upon capabilities to minimize learning curves for changes in the future. The longer/harder the transformation, the more likely that the capability you're building was not one you focused on previously. When you want to lose weight, you're likely out of shape and not living a healthy lifestyle. When you are looking for successors, you're likely losing top talent in your firm.

Nothing's wrong with building anew; you're just moving forward, armed with new skills to take on the challenge. Turning to reactionary behaviors, rather than developed capabilities, reinforces the anxiety associated with transformations. It's never too late to start a change. Managing behaviors consistently shortens the amount of transformational effort, personal analysis, and actions you need to take to make changes stick.

Your intention is to stay ready. That way when you experience other reasons to change, you can leverage your capabilities in the future and not necessarily start from scratch.

Nike famously marketed the slogan, *"There is no finish line."* You're continuously enhancing and integrating capabilities to meet the demands of an evolving tomorrow. As noted earlier, the characters and behaviors that served a purpose in your life may become outdated. Your capabilities for transformation are no different. Continue to build and strengthen your capabilities to transform and meet the demands of what's to come.

Now that you have the gift of knowledge, if you *stay* ready, you won't have to *get* ready. A lot of energy is used on getting you ready (i.e. starting from "0," creating a foundation on which to start, building those capabilities, slowing your progress by making the minimum effort, etc.), rather than having a place to springboard from. Having a foundation of capability, reinforced from use, allows you to stay ready.

That doesn't mean you will always have a place from which you can springboard. It does mean that you now know what to look for, where to start, and how to move through transformations that minimize the upfront work around discovery and getting to know yourself that is often mistakenly skipped during times of change.

It is not your capabilities that show who you truly are, it is the consistency of your choices and actions.

OPERATE WITH INTENTION: PAUSE. PROCESS. REFLECT.

You are nearing the conclusion of this book. Hopefully, you are changed in part by its contents and more by your discovery of capabilities to transform your story. From this self-discovery, you've received the gift of knowledge. You're living with a new awareness and principles to continue your transformative journey.

However, the knowledge of self and your capabilities will become stale and useless without continuous commitment, conviction, energy, and application. As with those practicing the violin or with athletes, sustainment requires intentional effort and focus to integrate capabilities into your routines, all to prepare for a ten-minute recital or the chance to push further on the next go-around at athletic competition. Otherwise, habits fall victim to resolutions that start, then fade with time.

A portion of your sustainment relies on perseverance through challenges that invariably will test your will. Your environment also influences sustainment, where "new" habits need friends for support, encouragement, and alignment.

Just when the caterpillar thought the world was over, it became a butterfly - Proverb

While sustainment is nice, it is not always necessary. Also important is separating the habits that you will sustain versus those that have served a specific purpose. Maybe you will find that only building a capability is enough, and a larger change is not required.

In either instance, you are still transforming your story. Consider:

1. What is your "again," an area in which you must build more repetition?

2. What capabilities/behaviors require refinement for sustainment?

3. What routines require updates so your "new" has friends?

4. How do decisions of what you are willing and not willing to do impact your ability to sustain this (these) new behavior(s)?

5. How can you maintain conscious awareness of you, your environment, and your actions for honest reflection and assessment?

6. Where do you require a pivot, so you can expand your target or move to next one?

Again, as Nike marketed, *"There is no finish line."* Continuously refining your capabilities over time allows you to stay ready for your next transformation.

CONCLUSION
AN OPEN LETTER

"No matter how far a person can go, the horizon is still way beyond you."
—Zora Neal Hurston

DEAR READER,

Your story is still being written.

Without another action, your story is wonderful. Filled with character, challenge, climax, reflection, and continuity, irrespective of any additional decision or movement. Yet, we are preset to continue writing our stories.

I started this book by asking, "What is the greatest ability of humans?" After much thought, what emerged as our greatest ability is our capacity to *evolve*. While a portion of our innate ability is controlled by the world, other portions of our evolution are controlled by our *choices*. In these instances, we have the opportunity to act intentionally by taking ownership of our stories.

From the outset, this book focused on your desire to change as a point of personal transformation. It advocates for building intentional focus around how to build the capability to transform – regardless of what may have caused your need –and assist you in progressing into an unknown future. Research has shown that capabilities are framed through symbols from our past, forethought, the self-regulation of emotions in the moment, personal reflection, and continuous learning.

The first capability focused on expanding your awareness beyond the challenges presented, through *Discovering* a deeper truth on what you were solving. Through the "dot" exercise, you uncovered more of the "chalkboard" than you saw previously. Focusing solely on the "dot" misses true causes of your need to change. As such, this refocused you on redefining your true target for transformation.

You then transitioned to explore symbols in your life that create the principles of you, irrespective of doing anything different. Similar to "grains of sand," you are more than the *chapter* of change where you *walked in*. Your characters, environment, and choices all played a role in *The Principle of You* and what you hoped to achieve.

This analysis fostered forethought that provided the foundation in creating your *Plan*. From your target, you identified actions to take, minimizing "tasks of futility" when "chasing" your target, and reducing decisions so you are not inundated with so much constant active thought that it causes mental exhaustion. You also considered your *return on enjoyment*. This was also the time to reflect on your environments impact, where you could plan for noise (similar to Remy dealing with his father's objections in *Ratatouille*) and discomfort. Combined, your *Plan* reframed success that focused on behaviors and incremental progress.

Each of these initial parts intentionally established a strategic lens on your transformation, ahead of taking action. While you enjoyed the *idea* of transformation, the initial steps in transforming your story began in earnest. You built the capability of *Experience*, focused on acting in the now and regulating emotions. Similar to bartenders, you sought experiences that *consolidated your movements* and allowed you to *make the cheap mistake*. As Lucy Maud Montgomery said, "Although ambitions are well worth having, they are not cheaply won." And while your "microphone" was different than mine, the practice of managing moments of transformations may be daunting, but it also offers points of reference on which to build.

While done throughout, you became *Attuned* with who you are by reflecting on progress and learning. You continuously reviewed progress, revising your plan, and becoming actualizing toward your transformation. If not, you may be constrained by decisions and an environment that will recast *darkness* on the *light* your transformation is intended *to repair*.

Compelling stories have moments that transform how you experienced the world. Your experience doesn't end, as *there is no finish line*. It is repeated, refined, and applied again, much like the preparation for a *violin recital*.

At its core, this book created an opportunity for you to acknowledge the person you were, the person you are, and take steps to be the person you want to be through a framework where you are the author, actor, and director of your story. Capabilities help manage your story's evolution, but it takes personal will to sustain them over time.

As the cycles of life and experience pass, it will become easier to manage the parts of your narrative you want changed with a sense of empowerment, confidence, and depth not experienced before. You may or may not have transformed completely, like a caterpillar to butterfly, but you started the process. And sometimes, that's good enough.

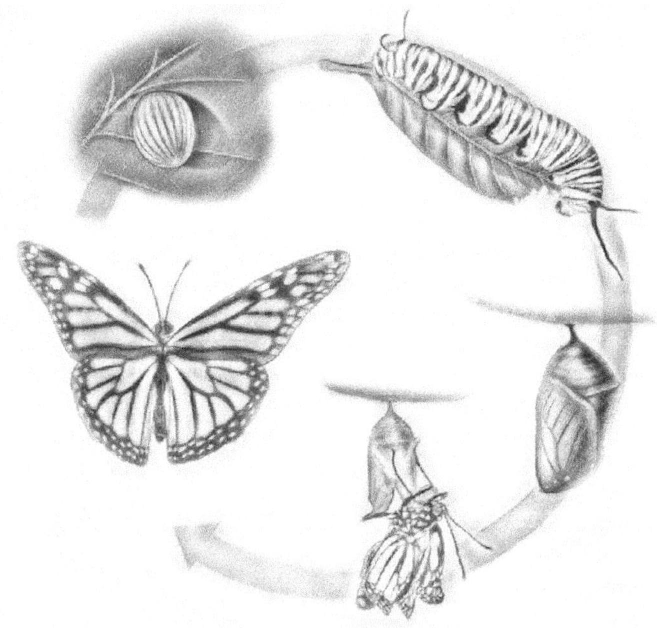

Keep moving forward as you continue to write your story...

"...because in the end, all you will remember is the story."
— Martin Aguilar, III

Leverage your gift of knowledge and exploration of self through the questions throughout this process when experiencing your next transformation. While you may come close to your horizon, it will always be slightly beyond you. Thank you for investing in yourself, as time and energy are precious commodities we don't get back.

Best of luck as you continue your evolution, as each moment offers an opportunity to build and refine your capabilities. If needed, I'll be here to help...

...with *Intention*.

Ian D. Brooks PhD, MS

ACKNOWLEDGMENTS

This book has been five-year journey that I could not have managed without help.

I benefited from my editor and book coach Robin Quinn of Quinn's Word for Word who reviewed each draft, answered questions, offered support, and provided insight into different ways of thinking across this writing. The value of her patience and coaching throughout this process has been immeasurable.

Thank you to Andi Dube from A Speedy Writer for providing a fresh lens on the final manuscript. She offered a view of the "chalkboard" in places where I was staring at the "dot."

Many thanks are also due to my direct support team. To Matt Belardi, who is the only person to have read and heard every version of this book's evolution. Thank you for your feedback and humoring me reading the early versions of this book. To all of my other friends who provided encouragement, offered feedback on early versions to enhance content, and continuously asked me about my progress to help keep me accountable. Each of you at times have brightened my day with laughter when I needed a break or has lent a listening ear during times of frustration. Thank you.

I also want to thank Lori Marple-Pereslete, Tony Pereslete, and Bill Navarrow, from Runkee Productions for their support, coaching, and laughter during the audiobook recording. This experience was a pivotal point in my transformation and allowing me to become the writer this book needed.

It is because of these wonderful individuals, and countless others, that I have been able to accomplish this goal. Thank you all.

WORKS CITED

PART I
Bandura, A. (1989). Human agency in social cognitive theory. *American Psychologist.* 44, 1175-1184.

PART II
von Oech, Roger. (1989). Creative Whack Pack. U.S. Games Systems Inc.)

Osborn, Alex. (1953). *Applied Imagination: Principles and Procedures of Creative Problem Solving.* New York, New York: Charles Scribner's Sons.

Miller, S.,Wackman, D. B., Nunnally, E. W., & Miller, P. (1992). *Connecting: With Self and Others.* Littleton, CO: Interpersonal Communication Programs.

PART III
Arkoff, A. (1995). *The Illuminated Life.* Needham Heights, MA: Simon & Schuster Company

PART IV
Deci, Edward. (1995). *Why We Do What We Do: Understanding Self-Motivation.* New York, New York: Penguin Books.

PART VI
Lindsley, D.H., Brass, D.J., & Thomas, J.B. (1995). Efficacy-performance spirals: A multilevel perspective. *Academy of Management Review,* 20(3), 645-678.

PART VII
Deci, Edward. (1995). *Why We Do What We Do: Understanding Self-Motivation.* New York, New York: Penguin Books.

ABOUT THE AUTHOR

Ian D. Brooks PhD, MS is the CEO/Founder of Rhodes Smith LLC. Since 2012 his consulting firm has helped people reach their potential and organizations engage employees and aligned them to business goals.

Prior to starting Rhodes Smith, Dr. Brooks worked for various Fortune 500 companies internally or as a consultant to improve individual stories for 25 years. His unique perspective combines experiences from clinical psychology, work within organizations, and being a human continuously evolving. He grew up in Sterling, VA and now lives in Los Angeles, CA.

For more about Dr. Brooks, visit rhodessmith.com or Twitter @DrB_Intention.

www.ingramcontent.com/pod-product-compliance
Lightning Source LLC
Chambersburg PA
CBHW051457050726
47593CB00005B/2115